William Waldorf Astor

Sforza

a story of Milan

William Waldorf Astor

Sforza
a story of Milan

ISBN/EAN: 9783743372689

Manufactured in Europe, USA, Canada, Australia, Japa

Cover: Foto ©ninafisch / pixelio.de

Manufactured and distributed by brebook publishing software (www.brebook.com)

William Waldorf Astor

Sforza

SFORZA

A STORY OF MILAN

BY

WILLIAM WALDORF ASTOR

AUTHOR OF "VALENTINO"

TO MY DEAR WIFE.

CONTENTS.

CHAPTER I.
The School of the Sword .... PAGE *1*

CHAPTER II.
Invasion *16*

CHAPTER III.
Isabelle of Aragon *35*

CHAPTER IV.
The Marriage of the Sea *53*

CHAPTER V.
The Star Chamber *73*

CHAPTER VI.
Between the Red Pillars 93

CHAPTER VII.
A Prophecy of the Stars 111

CHAPTER VIII.
A Revelation 129

CHAPTER IX.
The Hall of the Signoria 146

CHAPTER X.
Lago Lario 163

CHAPTER XI.
Festa dell' Ottobrata 180

CHAPTER XII.
Le Chevalier Bayard 199

CHAPTER XIII.
The Monastery of Divine Love 218

CHAPTER XIV.

	PAGE
An Alchemic Magnet	237

CHAPTER XV.

The Faith of the Swiss	257
Conclusion	275

SFORZA.

CHAPTER I.

THE SCHOOL OF THE SWORD.

A FINE breezy July morning had dawned upon Milan. At the market prevailed a hubbub of sounds that had begun with the arrival of the earliest contadini: before the inns, ostlers and servants chatted and laughed as they worked; at the half-finished Duomo, the people streamed in and out, pausing in the cool, incensed air of the aisles to touch a finger-tip in holy water; on the piazza d'armi, a regiment of gaudily-attired soldiers marched and wheeled with drumbeat and bugle-note; and along the quiet banks of the little Olona some boatmen towed and punted their barges with fantastic snatches of song.

The year 1499 had opened with lowering aspect. Louis the Twelfth of France, eager to efface the discredit of his arms, had avowed his purpose of scourging Ludovico Sforza, Duke of Milan, for a scheming adroitness which, five years before, had caused the military misfortunes of Charles the Eighth. To secure the advantage of a diversion upon his subtle antagonist, he had signed a treaty with the Venetians, whereby they were to make an irruption upon the frontier of Lombardy, while the French army, composed of knights, arquebusiers, Swiss pikemen, and an artillery train of thirty bronze cannon, should pass the Alps and cleave its way to Milan. The approach of so formidable a host might have gladdened the Milanese with the prospect of quick riddance of their usurping duke, but for the dread of men whose cruelties had touched half Italy with suffering; and so, as successive couriers announced the gathering of the French in Dauphiné, and their concentration in Piedmont, the fickle populace knew not whether to tremble or to rejoice.

Walking leisurely along one of the principal streets, with an eye to any bright face that might peep from gable or carved balcony, went a young man named Hermes Sforza, whose air and dress betokened him to be of the luxurious aristocracy. His costume was of striped blue and white satin, with a cap set with diamonds on his head; at his left wrist tinkled three slender bracelets, and his long hair was heavily perfumed and bound in a gauze net, after the fashion of Spain. He turned into an unfrequented by-way, down which an individual of much his own attire, though of more advanced age, came sauntering. A smile illumined Sforza's face at the sight, and, quickening his step, he saluted the other with patronizing effusion.

"Is it indeed you, Messer Bernardino?" he began, speaking his native Italian with a Spanish accent, which was the fashionable affectation of the period. "I am glad of our meeting; you shall tell me the news; you know I have been back but a day, therefore return a step with me; we will talk as we go. Narvaez awaits me—how I long to cross rapiers with him again!"

The individual thus addressed halted at the greeting, and answered with a smile:

"You look jovial as ever, Hermes; the moist English climate does not dampen the spirits, it seems."

"I feel dull this morning; I have been out the livelong night."

"And the little Rucellai with hazel eyes?"

"Tush, Bernardino, a truce to thy nonsense!"

"So you are going now to your fencing master's; and after that?"

"After that we shall breakfast together at the Osteria del Povero Diavolo—you know it not? Why, they tell me 'tis a new cookshop opened since I left, where everything is done to perfection in the Spanish style."

"My time is brief; I but meant to refresh myself with a breath of air."

"Diamine! you must eat; I will hasten my exercise. I have a hundred questions to ask, as all people have after separation."

"Are you, too, going to the army?" inquired Bernardino, turning to retrace his steps.

"For the present, no; I am attached to the military household. Doubtless we shall all look the French in the eyes before the next Ottobrata. But what of that! Tell me rather how to forget England. Maledetto! think of a whole month there."

"Is it true that in London the red-haired girls play games wherein they kiss the men?" inquired Bernardino, casting his eyes upon his companion's bangles and effeminate dress.

"Possibly, but not with strangers, and I was always a stranger among them."

"But at Carnival?"

"They buffet one another's faces with great gloves. But what carnival will you have when from Christmas to Easter the fog is so dense you would not know there were church towers did not you hear the tinkling of the chimes? I cannot yet shake off the impression of those grimy streets, of the rainy mornings, of the dark, solemn afternoons. And the faces at the diamond-paned windows! Always the weazened faces of old scriveners and money-changers, poring over their books and fumbling their hoards."

"They must needs drink well in such a climate?"

"Drink! 'Tis a country which makes no wine. They serve at their banquets a dry Xeres which they call sack, and the people play the fool in their cups over a frothing yellowish liquid."

"You talk as though you had been homesick."

"I had the longing for Italy, and that, you know, is a malady incurable abroad. I thought of the silver and gold of our sky, of the sunset flush on our mountains, of my favorite haunts——"

"And somewhat of the little Rucellai—no?"

"Jest not of her, or my good fortune will fly away."

"Your good fortune delights me. And when is the wedding feast?"

"I spoke with her last night. Her father's house was filled with dancers. I have known the old man for years,—who knows not the banker Rucellai? I danced a moresca with her; we strolled among tapestries and paintings; she offered me a sherbet; I coaxed her to accept a bracelet from my wrist; we walked down a terrace where were statues and fountains and colored lanterns, and where a company of lutes were playing the sweetest love songs, and oh, Bernardino! it came over me that I might meet my death in this accursed war!"

"And that is all?"

"Hark. The dance over, the guests scattered,

the house closed, and, the night listening, I came with my mandolin and filled the air with song."

"You never used to sing."

"No; but love inspired me and gave me a voice; do you remember that quaint old passionate refrain of the Sunbeam and the Rose?"

"You are too sleek and too well fed, my Hermes, to be a soulful minstrel."

"So thought old Rucellai. A casement opened, and I recognized his voice. 'Begone,' he cried, 'if you are human you should have some compassion; if you are a devil I will presently discharge an arquebuse your way."

"And the girl?"

"Gave no sign. So, with the daughter asleep and the father awake, I betook me to a trattoria, where a dozen we know were supping, and presently in came a bevy of girls who danced for us—and here I am."

Their talk was interrupted by the leisurely round of a town-crier. He stopped near them, rang a bell, and, pointing to a handcuffed prisoner, recited the following words in a monotonous chant, while the culprit, a miserable starveling, with every token of degradation, listened intently, as though each repetition of the sentence brought a new horror:

"Be it known, that this man, Agosto Felice, a Jew, having been convicted of sweating the public moneys, and his goods forfeited, is condemned to be branded on the face and hands to-morrow."

The knot of idlers, that followed the trembling criminal throughout the city, passed on, and Hermes and Bernardino resumed their way unconcerned.

"Had the duke news yesterday from the army?" asked the latter.

"I saw my uncle but briefly; he looked pale and troubled, though, in answer to the only question I durst put to him, he said that all goes for the best. Nevertheless, twenty-five days since, as I was leaving London, it was told me by a secretary to the Pope's legate that the Venetians would assail us from behind. And at Como a rumor had it that their scappoli and stradiotes are already concentrated to march. Can such evil tidings be true?"

"'Tis but the accustomed bluster of the Venetians. Our forces assemble at Asti; it is to be a defensive campaign until our autumn fevers exhaust the French. At the worst, cannot our towns stand siege? If we but keep the French at arms' length for the summer, we shall make them eat bitter bread with cold hands."

They had now reached the abode of Narvaez, the celebrated fencing-master. There was an enclosure at one side where, in summer, he received his pupils *al fresco*, and here he had marked out upon the brick pavement the geometric lines which served as a basis for the theories of his school. From one extremity to the other ran parallels, along which, said a naïve explanation, two adversaries might travel without changing distance. Further on was an illustration, by footmarks, of the successive positions occupied in gaining the advantage of place and stroke by traversing. On the wall was the outline of a human figure, upon which were drawn, for the consideration of the beginner, lines showing the relation of angles to arcs, of tangents and chords to their circle.

Four hundred years ago every master of fence advocated a system developed by his own favorite methods. If he could afford the cost, he had copied for sale, in manuscript, his treatise upon staccadoes and imbrocatas and mandritas, mixed with disquisitions upon self-defence as approved by divine law, and on the commendable pastime of the sword for the confusion of heretics and the admiration of fair women. Some adepts offered to sell a *botte secrète*, a thrust that would surely reach the adversary, while others devoted themselves to pure theory, such as the exchange of compliments which Spanish etiquette provided before a duel; thence leading the scholar to the habitual study of every swordsman, whether stout, tall, muscular, nervous, choleric, or phlegmatic, with the inferential reasoning that such an opponent should be met with tactics violent, measured, sudden, or patient—and finally passing into philosophical digressions and the recital of Scriptural texts. That, in spite of such drawbacks, the Spaniards should have been accounted the most formidable duellists of the sixteenth century, was due to the strength required for the manipulation of their heavy rapier which its incessant use in practice developed, and to the habit of extreme coolness which resulted from unflagging attention to artificial method.

Both these qualities were possessed in their perfection by Narvaez, the renowned fencing-teacher, who advanced to greet Hermes and Bernardino as a servant admitted them into the enclosure. All Milan knew the young Spanish swordsman by sight. He had come to Italy when a stripling, and, since his father's death, had continued alone in the exercise of the family profession. The elder Narvaez had served his apprenticeship in arms when, as a boy, he stood by his father on the trembling rampart of Constantinople, and saw Paleologus cast aside the purple robe, that his body might not be recognized by the Saracens as that of the last of the Roman Cæsars.

His son inherited his deftness with the rapier, and the nerve of the professional swordsman. He had a serious face, a soft, musical voice, unusual in a Spaniard, thick clustering hair, an earnest manner in talking, and a smile as sweet as a girl's. His features were delicate, and under his dark skin glowed a ruddy flush. He was a favorite with all; with Hermes chiefly for his incomparable swordsmanship, and partly, be it confessed, because the fencer loved dainty dishes as much as though they were not contrary to perfect training. Half a dozen times, in bygone days, had Hermes taken him to one of his favorite resorts, where they had feasted magnificently, to the Spaniard's delight and to the promotion of a comradeship which in olden times often existed between a crack fencing-master and his patron.

But, above all, he was a favorite with the women —too much so for his own comfort. He declared the pursuit of the sex to be inconsistent with the pure science of the sword, and neither art nor cajolery nor amorous token could move his indifference. His most demonstrative admirer was a handsome widow of thirty, with ample revenue and a tendency to *embonpoint*. This dame had taken advantage of the prevalent taste among ladies for fencing, to gain a more particular acquaintance than the Spaniard usually permitted; but when she presumed upon this privilege with a sudden embrace and an impassioned declaration, the cold swordsman turned from her rosy face with a vow that he would never cross rapiers with her again.

"Good morning, Narvaez," said Hermes, "I present you to Messer Bernardino Corte, Governor of the Castle; doubtless he has seen you fence in public," he added, as the Spaniard raised a Moorish cap and bowed to his visitors with the grave courtesy of the profession.

"The maestro has perhaps never noticed my face," observed Bernardino, "though, Narvaez, I have often watched you,— the last time at that famous assalto wherein you vanquished the French champion."

The fencer begged Bernardino to seat himself at a bench embowered in vines, whence, while awaiting Sforza's return, he could observe the lesson progressing between an assistant and a youth receiving his first notions of arms. Bernardino glanced at the opposite wall, whereon was painted the maxim of the Cavaliere San Giorgio, of blessed memory: "To the heart, always strike at the heart," which the master was wont to repeat as he placed a sword in the scholar's hand; then his eyes rested upon the assistant as he repeated to his pupil the rules of posture, the respective merits of passing one or two fingers over the quillons, and the most approved method of advancing at an angle, with short, quick steps, always menacing the adversary with the point, and delivering upon the body of an imaginary opponent a stab-like thrust, which, in the use of the heavy Spanish rapier, took the place of the modern fencer's lunge.

Bernardino's musing was ended by the return of Hermes, who had exchanged his dainty clothes for a pair of coarse knee-breeches and a light shirt, over which was strapped a heavy plastron. In his right hand he carried a practising rapier with a small metal ball at the end, and in his left a mask. Narvaez gloved his right hand and bound a leather thong about his fingers and through the quillons with mathematical nicety, and they crossed swords. For twenty minutes Bernardino watched them, observing the careful poise of the heavy blades, the nimble feet, the exact balance of the body, the feint, the parry,—then the fencing humor seized him, and he longed for a bout himself. When Hermes stopped to rest, he approached, and, pointing to a rack of masks and blunt foils, said to Narvaez:

"Good youth, do me the service to make me breathe deep, and, if you touch me, I will call myself your pupil."

"Five ducats to one he pinks thee, Bernardino!" cried Hermes, as the governor threw off his slashed doublet and selected a sword.

Bernardino forced the fencing, thinking thereby to derive advantage from his superior weight and reach. Narvaez essayed to disengage, but his opponent's weapon always returned to contact with his own. At length he succeeded in dropping his sword ere his antagonist's blade caught it, and, with a turn of the wrist, delivered a stroke that touched Bernardino fairly on the breast.

"Well played, my Narvaez, and an honest Spanish mandoble," cried Hermes, laughing at his companion's defeat; "to the heart, always to the heart," he added, pointing to the maxim of the patron of fencers.

The governor appeared nettled. "If thou canst touch me again with such trifling care," he exclaimed, "I will reward the stroke with five gold ducats!"

Forward and back they moved, until Narvaez, abandoning his guarded defence, made several rapid passes, then, springing aside and forward, he executed the favorite manœuvre of the Spanish school, the traverse, to be followed by a thrust from the angle thus gained; but Bernardino resorted simultaneously to a counter of French invention, with the result that Narvaez, divining his thought, changed his own stroke in the instant of execution, and, catching his opponent's blade with his own, sent it flying to the ground.

At this discomfiture the governor turned on his heel in vexation, and drew on his doublet.

"Disarmed is worse than touched, and here are your five ducats," he said to the fencer, who dropped them into a purse which he tossed in the air with a merry laugh, and snatched as it descended. In a moment more Hermes had resumed his ordinary attire.

"And now for breakfast," pursued the governor, as they passed out into the street. "Fried pig's trotters, peppered kidneys, ham with olive sauce, eggs with cheese of Seville——"

His words ceased as the speaker crossed the path of an approaching individual, whose appearance caused him a disagreeable surprise. The newcomer was a man in the prime of life, of vigorous body and calm, intellectual face. He saluted Hermes and Bernardino with a slight wave of the hand and a murmured *buon giorno*, and pursued his leisurely way. Hermes, in returning his greeting, made, with middle fingers and thumb drawn together and fore and little fingers extended, the familiar sign which averts the blight of the evil eye.

"What brings Almodoro back?" he murmured. "He has been in the Levant for years, and I thought we were rid of him forever. Madre beatissima, my appetite is gone."

"He returned a week ago in answer to a pressing summons, and is now in high favor. We meet to-day at noon, and together are to be received by the duke. 'Tis said he has been on a pilgrimage."

"How should one who holds converse with Satan make a pilgrimage?"

"To confer with the evil spirits of the East — they are most potent under that burning sun. Behold!" added Bernardino, pointing to the ground, "mark you that—a dead leaf—whence comes it thus withered? See, it moves and rustles, though not a breath stirs."

"And, mark you, he is not aged a day since I last saw him. His looks never change. That is where you may read the devil's blessing. It is well known that he is Giacomo Contarini, aged forty-nine to-day —aged forty-nine when he was——"

"Bah! Giacomo Contarini was Doge of Venice half a dozen generations back."

"But he did not die."

"He resigned his office."

"Resigned his office and its burdens, left Venice, and has been wandering from one country to another ever since. In the doge's palace hangs his portrait among all the others. I have seen it, and it is Almodoro's face—the meeting eyebrows, the furtive look of the eyes, the sad, set expression of the lips, all are there—and yet that portrait of him was painted as he looked two centuries ago!"

CHAPTER II.

INVASION.

On a broad terrace that skirted the parapet of the castle of Milan sat Bernardino Corte, governor of that fortress, and Almodoro, soothsayer to the duke, and famous in the arts of magic and divination. Both were men of striking appearance. Bernardino possessed the muscular, deep-chested frame and easy poise of an athlete. He had fine gray eyes that could be keen or tender; his address was frank and engaging; for men, he had brief, clear, straightforward words, and for women the fascination of a handsome and successful man who apparently has never loved. His early years had been filled with adversity. He had travelled extensively, and, returning to his native Lombardy, brought back a large observation upon the tactics and equipment of foreign armies, and a mind filled with the poesy and romance of France and Spain. He could tell many a story of the age which produced "Le Roman de la Rose," and a novelette which he wrote attracted the attention of the Court.

Almodoro's was a more thoughtful face. He had

the vigorous physique and nerve-calm which remain when the mind has not been overtasked nor the body over-indulged. He seemed in the prime of life, a student in appearance, and, from his distrait look, one could divine a man habituated to the luxury of solitude. The repose and serenity of his presence indicated a life apart from ordinary care. His swarthy complexion had been deepened by Asiatic climates, and in his accent there was a savor of Oriental tongues. Of late he had been journeying in India, amid scenes with which he professed himself familiar, and in whose weird inspiration he delighted. Men said that he belonged to the brotherhood of alchemists—a connection which, with his learning and his independence, procured him the enmity of the Church,—an enmity whereof he might have received emphatic token had not the powers of darkness and of light been so evenly balanced in the estimation of the fifteenth century, that it was often accounted hazardous to meddle with the devil's own.

These two were the most trusted of all who, after aiding Ludovico Sforza in the dispossession of his nephew Galeazzo, had served him in the maintenance of his usurped authority. Their desultory talk had lapsed to silence as they awaited the summons which should presently call them to the presence of the duke, and they now sat with heads bared in the shade of an awning, while their gaze rested carelessly upon the castle enclosure, the clustering masses of tawny gables and peaked roofs, or, beyond, upon the immeasurable expanse of green, stretching away to the Alps, whose shadowy outline a keen eye could discover.

The famous citadel of Milan enclosed an extensive area, and served the purpose of palace, fortress, dungeon, treasury, and barrack. Within it resided the duke; at one side was imprisoned, with her child, Isabelle of Aragon, widow of the dispossessed Galeazzo: in a central tower were gold and precious stones. Along the rampart, ready to meet the impending attack, were stored the best appliances known to military science. Upon each tower was a contrivance capable of tossing a fifty-pound stone two hundred yards; within the covered galleries were ranged crossbows of such power that they could only be bent by a wheel; these last weapons threw either sharp steel bolts, to pierce the armor of a knight, or bars bound about with oakum dipped in inextinguishable fire, and were so deadly that the Council of the Lateran condemned them as "displeasing to God." In an angle of the wall was an immense copper pan, which, when filled with water and placed in the dry ditch or on the counterscarp, revealed the mines the enemy might be digging,—each blow of the pick in a subterranean gallery causing a quiver on the water.

"How tedious grows this waiting!" the governor ejaculated, unbuckling his sword and laying it on the bench beside him; "this morning's estaffette must have brought despatches of importance."

"Our couriers from Asti can bring only good tidings," answered Almodoro, "for we know that there all goes well; but I dread our next letters from Venice."

"Let us dismiss Venice from our thoughts, and bid Ludovico do likewise. The Senate threatens an incursion, and seeks to profit by the weakness which an unlucky year imposes on us; but the only real danger is that we should be beguiled into diverting a fraction of our strength from the decisive encounter with the French."

"Then what is to prevent the Venetians from marching upon Milan?" asked Almodoro. "You will say because they are Italians, and that, beyond the greed of adding a couple of towns to their Venetia, they would not help the invader. But I tell you the Venetians are not Italians: they are a people by themselves; they have more interests in the Levant, or along the narrow seas, than here."

"It seems to me," observed the governor after a pause, "that Ludovico is changed of late; ten years ago he would not have been taken thus, in evil days, with two powerful adversaries closing upon him, and not a friend in the world."

"Do you think it strange," retorted the soothsayer, "that a man should be disconcerted at the prospect of an exchange of rank and riches for odium and exile?"

"It is indeed a long way from his present elevation to the days of his condottiere ancestor," answered Bernardino, with a sneer.

"All my life," pursued the alchemist,—"and my life has been longer than my looks tell—I have watched people pass from one calamity to another; therefore I have ceased to marvel at the infinitely sad things Time brings about."

"And I," rejoined the governor, "who am younger in heart than in years, have but lately begun to wonder at them. Ah, mercy me! yesterday brought back a bitter memory. Were you in Milan, Almodoro, fourteen years ago, when the plague was at its worst? No? Well I was here. The streets were deserted; every other lintel bore the red sign; the dead-cart passed with its crucifix and its ghastly burden. I fled from the infected air, and from the horrors that thronged on every side. In all the streets I saw but one person, a youth of my own age. I recall his face with vividness, though we met no more until two years after, when he took from me a girl of whom I was enamoured. It was a boyish amourette of mine, and foolish, if you will; but such follies are the part of life one loves best to look back upon. We crossed swords in a grove beyond Monza, and by way of satisfaction I received two inches of his rapier. I came out of the delirium of a sick-room to learn that he and my sweetheart were married. Twelve years have passed since then, and yesterday, going into the Duomo to rest my thoughts in the calm of its great white arches, I heard a priest chanting, and saw a knot of people before the altar, and in their midst a bier, and the face of the dead was uncovered; and I looked, and recognized my rival."

"You did not weep for him," remarked the soothsayer indifferently.

"You might have thought I wept, for the tears welled up to my eyes, and I lost the glittering altar, and the droning priest, and the dead face, and it seemed to me that I looked across them all to the last time that I saw *her*, and I remembered the crimson flush of that beautiful day, and the tinkling cadenças of guitars, and it all came over me like a new sorrow."

"'Tis true that an old wound sometimes bleeds afresh," assented Almodoro, restraining an inclination to smile at his companion's unwonted earnestness. "The Arabs call it *the cut of a poisoned knife*. But hither comes a page to summon us."

Before receiving his confidential advisers Ludovico Sforza had dined, as usual, at midday and alone. In a room painted with Moorish arabesques, a major-domo, attended by two servants, stood beside a table laid with damask cloth, and furnished with knife and spoon and wooden salt-cellar, and Dutch porcelain platter, and tinted goblet of Murano. They waited but a moment, for Sforza had that punctuality which in olden times was the virtue of princes.

A curtain was thrown back and the duke entered. Though grown portly, Sforza was still of erect, graceful figure. His face was full, clean-shaven, of dark complexion, with a profile suggestive of firmness and refinement. His lips were delicate and expressive. His eyes were black, lustrous, and piercing, and looked from beneath strongly-arched brows. His hair was cut square in front, and brushed forward half way down the forehead, and worn long at the sides and back. In character he was shaped according to Macchiavelli's subsequent standard of princely excellence,—astute, self-reliant, well-informed, cruel at times, though less through badness of heart than in compliance with the stern egotism of the time, and using fraud and force with the subtleness of Italian statecraft. He was indefatigable in advancing the welfare of his subjects, fond of letters and of the companionship of learned men, and a magnificent patron of the arts. His sagacity had procured him the sobriquet of "Il Moro," *the mulberry tree*, which, being in spring the last to hazard its buds and the first to mature its fruit, he had adopted as his symbol of patience and promptness. Of recent years he had been saddened by the death of his young wife, Beatrice; if he had sought to console himself for this affliction, it had been chiefly in the society of scholars, in the employment of Bramante and Da Vinci, and in the development and better cultivation of Lombardy.

He seated himself without heeding the majordomo's formal reverence, which, at the commencement of each meal, conveyed the assurance that the dishes had been watched and the wine tasted, and that, under Providence, neither had been tampered with. From the sideboard were brought long, slender stems of bread and a bowl of the famous "golden soup," made of saffron and the yolk of eggs, for it was Friday, and the duke was scrupulous in fasting. To tunny, browned and laid on a bed of parsley, succeeded macaroni, simmered beans, and toasted cheese, the servants being careful, in deference to a superstition of the time, to approach the table with the right foot first. Having finished this frugal repast, Il Moro returned to his library, where he had been at work all the morning. This was a large oblong room with easy-chairs and divans, and a great carved writing-table; on two sides were bookshelves flanked by salient caryatids, and between the windows hung a map of the world as then known, with curious beasts depicted upon the African coast, and still stranger monsters rising from the Sinus Barbaricus of the Indian Ocean; in frames, whose gilding had faded to a subdued lustre, were portraits of bygone Sforza,—intent and meditative men, and women subtle-eyed; here and there, beneath them, were black cabinets with inlaid panels and chased handles and ivory figures, that age had streaked with russet; the casements were set in deep niches, and through their little painted panes the sunlight laid a kaleidoscopic pattern upon the floor.

The duke's eyes fell on a clock that stood before the table, and which, in that day, was a rare curiosity; apparently reminded by its quaint face, he ordered that his nephew, Hermes, be called, and, upon his entrance, he saluted him with cold civility and bade him be seated.

"You find me," he began, abruptly, after a quick glance at the bright, manly face, "in even graver straits than when I ordered your recall from England."

He paused, seemingly in expectation of an answer; but his nephew's remembrance of years of neglect and isolation was too vivid to permit even the semblance of a sympathy he could not feel, and he received this declaration in silence.

"More than once," resumed the duke, coming to the subject in his thought, "you have reproached me for the seclusion of Francesco and his mother.

In the past it has been difficult to answer, except to ask if you would put Milan in the care of a child, or to repeat to you the words with which I have sought to quiet my own conscience, that, if aught has been done amiss, it is too late to turn back, and as for regrets and repinings, they are for women. You see I speak frankly, and in this hour of danger I acknowledge that I have been unjust, and I declare that so far as lies in my power I will make amends."

The young man shook his head incredulously. "You cannot bring back my dead brother," he said, with bitterness; "you will not release Isabelle; you think the French less dangerous to you than little Francesco."

"But at least I have at heart the welfare—what say I?—the salvation—of our family; and in this, if upon nothing else, we should agree."

"But we do not understand alike the interest of our family," retorted Hermes, with barely perceptible sarcasm. "For you, that interest is that, while you rule Milan, I am to be sent on distant and useless missions, and Isabelle and her boy are to be kept soften the word as you please—in a prison."

The duke checked him with a vehement gesture. "Be these rights and grievances what they may," he exclaimed "we shall all presently be outcasts together."

"And whose the fault?" bluntly ejaculated his nephew. "Did not every one but Almodoro tell you at the time that to call the French into Italy would, in the end, prove fatal? You opened the Alps a dozen years ago to Charles the Eighth—and now, here are the French on a second foray; and how must we, who bring such devastation, be regarded?"

"Your words are stern, Hermes, but I have said as much to myself. Let us think no more of what happened years ago; a thousand regrets are not worth a single archer, and one lucky day may right months of mistakes and misfortunes. I began by declaring that I would atone for the wrong done in my name, in exchange for a service it is in your power to render—not me individually, but our family."

"A service that I am to render!"

"Do you refuse?"

"First let me hear what it is?"

"We are ruined if the advance of the Venetians continue; the French we can meet, but not both together. You have a strong interest at stake, and what I ask is that you go to Venice, see the doge, and deliver to him a letter which I dare not trust to other hands."

"What has this to do with the atonement you spoke of?"

"That for its successful performance I will grant

what you have so often asked, and liberate Isabelle and Francesco."

"For this I will carry a letter to whom you will. I grieve whenever I see that forlorn little boy. And the duchess! I would give a year of life to free her, if only because it was I who commanded her escort hither from Naples, and once, in the midst of many sorrows, she said with an intensity of reproach that rings in my ears, *It was you who brought me to this unhappy place!*'"

"Then we are agreed already. But I do not conceal from you that this is a difficult and dangerous adventure, for every one knows that it is treason to Venice for the doge to receive such a letter."

"By the keys of St. Peter, you send me upon a thorny quest."

"Bunglers are caught; a clever fellow slips between obstacles that, for the moment, are no better than watchmen asleep."

"How will it be possible to reach the doge?"

"Easily enough. Their great festival of the Marriage of the Sea has this year been postponed from Ascension Day, first by stormy weather, then by Barbarigo's illness, till now it is fixed for three days hence. At that holiday all Venice is topsy-turvy, the attention of the council and of the signori di notte, as they call their police, is relaxed. For half a day the doge is comparatively a free man—it is not supposed he can conspire with the

Adriatic. And in that hour of celebration, amid the merrymaking that surrounds the Bucentoro, is your opportunity."

"And I am to give him your letter."

"Yes, I shall give you two letters,—this little triangular note for Barbarigo, and the other, as a last resort, for his brother who serves him as secretary, and who, if the worst befall, and you are forced to see the doge at his private palace, will procure an audience."

"And if I am detected . . . ?"

"Beware of that. The Venetians watch their doge as though he were a state prisoner, and it entails terrible risks for a stranger to visit him secretly. That is why I urge you to slip it him in the crowd as though it were a petition, for its form has a significance, and will warn him that it is no ordinary paper. Then your task is done and you disappear in the throng."

"And for this service you promise to let Isabelle and Francesco go their ways whithersoever they please."

"I not only promise it to you, but I will so declare it to them this very day."

"Then I am ready: but tell me, why select me for this difficult adventure?"

"Because, in spite of our differences, there is none other I dare so fully trust."

"And what says this letter?"

"That which will fly straight to the heart of Barbarigo."

"You do not expect me to go alone?"

"Would you take a troop of horse? You are to personate a banker's clerk commissioned with a transfer of moneys. I have had notes made ready, that you might be equipped to sustain your character."

"The man I have in thought is a tried swordsman of coolness and courage."

"And his name?"

"Narvaez, my master of fence."

"Take, then, your fencer, but bid him be sober and silent. Here are your letters, a memorandum of instructions you are to read, a purse of ducats, and a map of the way. Provide your own horses, leave to-morrow, and remember that the unforeseen always happens."

A few moments later Almodoro and Bernardino Corte were shown into the duke's presence for the conference which, during the last fortnight, had been part of the daily routine. Several members of this improvised council were absent; Sanseverino, the commander-in-chief, was away with the army. Landriano, the high treasurer, was absorbed in his finances; and Cardinal Ascanio Sforza, unwilling to brook longer the influence of two men whom he considered, the one a juggling trickster, and the other a mere soldier of parades, had betaken himself in disgust to other duties.

The duke seated himself upon a long divan intended for the afternoon siesta, and called a "lit de repos." Almodoro placed himself at the writing-table, and Bernardino, jealous as the cardinal of the alchemist, sat a little apart with face half averted.

"I have called you," began the duke, spreading some despatches upon his knees, "to consider first Landriano's answer to the question how to draw the utmost support from the populace. He declares that the thousands that fill the streets with mischievous talk should be employed upon the public works. He reminds me that the canals which drain the rice fields are unfinished, and says half a million ducats to keep the idle busy were money well spent."

"Does he think," asked Almodoro with a disparaging air, "that the city will continue quiet because a fraction of laborers are drawing pay?"

"It is the fraction you sneer at," answered Bernardino, "which strikes the spark and sets the firewood blazing."

"At best," retorted the soothsayer, indifferent to the governor's ill humor, "Landriano's is a threadbare answer. The duke needs money in his treasury, not out of it, and soldiers—not an army of shovellers."

"As for money," observed the governor coolly, "it must come as usual, by way of a loan from the nobles and burgesses."

"You can more lightly talk of such a loan than I dare order it," replied Ludovico with a shake of the head.

"Then call the Signoria, as the cardinal suggested, and tell the situation in straightforward words."

"Can I demand money and make explanations in this stress to a roomful of jealous nobles, with a discontented rabble in the street?"

"It were still more hazardous to let the Venetians approach Milan."

"I have thought," said Sforza, cunningly, "of a resort which may prevent the Venetian advance."

At these words Bernardino changed his nonchalant attitude and eyed the duke intently, eager to hear what this project might be; but the disclosure was prevent d by an interruption from Almodoro.

"Then speak it not," exclaimed the alchemist with the familiarity of an intimate adviser; "it is needless for us to know aught beyond our individual duty; and if a caution be required at this time, behold—here are the names of twelve reputable citizens now in correspondence with the enemy."

Ludovico's dark face flushed as he snatched the paper; then he hesitated, while the governor observed him in silence; at length, after a moment's indecision, he tossed it into the soothsayer's lap.

"Take back your list," he said; "it is now no time to punish, and I suffer enough without having in mind all the men who wish me ill. Keep it till autumn; then, if I still live, bring it me again."

"At least," cried Bernardino, angrily addressing Almodoro, "you will tell the source from which you derive those names. I wonder," he added, half to himself, "on whom your next suspicion will fall." Then, without waiting for an answer, he turned impatiently and began toying with the amber figures of a chess table that stood within reach.

"My suspicion rests upon intercepted letters, which I am ready to produce," replied the alchemist, addressing Sforza. Then, glancing at Bernardino, he added significantly, "Is that sufficient?"

At this declaration the governor turned from his chessmen, and observed with a careless gesture: "There is never a siege without disaffected, and what can these twelve do more than talk for themselves?" Then, speaking with sudden vehemence, he cried: "It is little we need think of Milan; the castle overawes the populace; you have, you say, an expedient whereby to save the city from the Venetians; then our exclusive care should be for

Sanseverino's army; that it be not exposed through his rashness; that it be used in such defensive manner as to gain time; that, above all, we withstand the temptation to recall some part of it for our needs here."

"This despatch, written yesterday," answered Ludovico, "shows how skilfully the army is disposed to watch the enemy, while keeping out of reach."

"Is not Landriano coming to the castle to-day?" asked Ahnodoro.

"No; he is busy settling arrears."

"Then let him take to-morrow also to sound the bankers about a loan to the treasury, and, if they talk of security, give them a mortgage on the lands of the Church."

"Cardinal Ascanio would invoke the anathema of St. Peter, if he heard you."

"Then pledge the coffers of the Jews."

"Ungrateful rogues! At the first whisper of war they removed their money bags out of the country by a scurvy trick called bills of exchange."

Ludovico interrupted them with an impatient wave of the hand. "Landriano shall talk to the usurers," he said; then, addressing Bernardino, he added: "One of the contractors of supplies has somewhat to complain of, and waits below at the rail. I pray you speak with him and let me know to-morrow what he asks."

At this the governor withdrew to a chamber, where the individual referred to waited on the other side of an iron grating, which Ludovico's fear of assassination put between himself and ordinary persons.

Almodoro also went his ways, and the duke was left alone.

He was still glancing over his reports when a paper of unfamiliar appearance caught his eye. Within it was written in a strange hand:

"*Bernardino puts the torch to your paradise.*"

CHAPTER III.

ISABELLE OF ARAGON.

Il Moro's interviews with his nephew and with his chief counsellors disposed of, he busied himself with his secretaries until a late hour in the day, when, taking up a silk cap and cloak, he crossed the great courtyard to the residence wherein were lodged the captive duchess and her child.

This woman is presented by contemporary writers as intelligent, beautiful, and accomplished; but especially as one of the most ill-fortuned characters of Italian history. Brought at the age of seventeen from her seaside home at Bari, she was married, at the instance of her grandfather, King Ferdinand of Naples, to Galeazzo Sforza, heir to the duchy of Milan. This prince had at that time been for nine years under the tutelage of his uncle, whose regency was evidently intended to become permanent.

Stung at length to decided speech by the appeals of his granddaughter, King Ferdinand bade Ludovico relinquish the honors he usurped, or accept the alternative of war. To this menace the duke replied by proposing to Charles the Eighth of France to possess himself of the kingdom of Naples; and the French king, fired with an ardor for conquest, soon after crossed the Alps and extinguished the Neapolitan house of Aragon. Ludovico often exulted at this discomfiture, and the rapidity and completeness of his ingenious stroke made him the envy and the admiration of his neighbors. The main purpose of the French accomplished, he profited by their reverses to join with the Venetians in obliging them to an inglorious retreat. In the midst of these events the young Galeazzo died, thereby rendering Ludovico's triumph complete.

Upon this catastrophe Isabelle withdrew to Pavia, where she abandoned herself to uncontrolled grief. But fate had further ills in store, the first of which was her compulsory return to the castle of Milan, in a captivity no longer disguised, and ever haunted by the dread that she and her child might presently suffer the violent end which mediæval statecraft meted out to the heirs of a fallen foe.

In a seclusion only troubled by bugle call or by the movement of equerries and guards, Isabelle passed five weary years. By day, when the pageant of morning drill was over, the inmates of the castle passed their time in idleness as vacant as the calm of a cloister. In the warm noontide a lethargy settled upon rampart and courtyard, and at night the changing of the sentinels, or the faint halloo of some roysterer without the walls, or on state occasions a murmur of revels, were the only sounds. Her short career was to her a story of hateful memories. She had loved, and her youth had been full of bright promise; disappointment and humiliation had taught her to suffer with patience; and when Galeazzo died, and the overthrow of her family at Naples left her alone and helpless, the world had darkened around her with the shadows of a changeless twilight.

For an hour each day she was allowed to walk within the castle enclosure, followed at respectful distance by a halberdier. She chiefly sought a retired angle of the rampart, where, through long years of peace, a dozen century plants had been allowed to grow in great old flower-pots, while beside them, and in contrast to their thorny and ancient blades, sprouted the tendrils and buds of to-day. Here she would sit while her child played ball against the rosy brick façade of the keep, or scampered in pursuit of a huge dog which was his inseparable companion; and here, in reveries less poignant than the memory of her departed splendor, she retraced the days of her girlhood at Bari, and walked again by the murmuring Adriatic, and listened to the sadness and the secrets of the sea. In such hours she loved to recall the crisp salt breeze, and the foaming billows, and the argosies vanishing upon the horizon. Often her fancy had followed these passing vessels upon wonderful cruises, and her imagination, dwelling upon narratives of Oriental journeyings, could picture the luxuriant beauty of the Levant as though the touch of some new Aladdin's lamp had kindled its enchanted brilliance. And even now the fabled East, which had filled so many early days, still haunted these heavy years of imprisonment. For beside the bench whereon she rested was a Saracenic sundial, which, in a bygone generation, had been the gift of a Genoese merchant to some departed Sforza. Time and exposure had chipped and stained its rich *giallo* marble, in whose centre a caliph of Bagdad had written a thought of the transiency of earthly things, that could both moderate the excess of joy and soften the edge of sorrow:

"And this, too, shall pass away!"

Often had Isabelle mused over the blurred tracery of this solemn inscription, with a wondering speculation upon the life by whose failures it must have been suggested. In what enchanted garden of the Orient had this tablet rested ages ago? How many thousands must have lingered to read its melancholy admonition! With how enduring a voice did the caliph speak from the tomb, and with how profound a truth of the yearning of inexperience, and of the bereavement of age!

Unconscious of the visit she was presently to receive, Isabelle had prepared to pass the evening with her fancy work, seated, as usual, in a boudoir which looked upon the courtyard, and which was flanked on one side by an oratory, and on the other by a sleeping-room, whose open door permitted a glimpse of a great high bed hung with draperies of sarcenet that fell on each side of the little flight of steps by which the couch was reached. There was small semblance of luxury about this modest lodging; the tiled floor was uncovered; in the middle of the room was a table, and here, beneath a cluster of lights, the boy Francesco was eating a bowl of porridge by the side of his mother. Isabelle had turned in listlessness from the tapestry which stood before her with its half-finished shapes of stately promise, and sky of enchanted coloring, and tracery of branches with rare and fabled fruit.

In a corner, and evidently neglected, leaned an ivory lute of exquisite workmanship, with curved neck bent like the throat of a swan, and about it a ribbon that had figured on many a brilliant evening when the duchess had touched her instrument and brought from its singing strings the wild and sweet and languorous melodies of her Neapolitan home. Before her, and covering the unused fireplace, stood a damask screen which, in the first months of her married life, Isabelle had embroidered with the familiar amaranths of her garden. It was one of her few mementos of those remote and short-lived days; and now, in the solitude and silence of her captivity, and amid the sombre recollections that pursued her, those faded little flowers seemed the blossoms of a lost and incomparable summer. On the wall above hung a sketch of herself, taken when a child playing by the seaside at Bari, with the rippling Adriatic at her feet, and, in the offing, an argosy sailing magnificently away beneath towering canvas. The sight of this picture brought only heartburn and an infinite compassion, and yet it was the most cherished of all her humble possessions. But to Franceschino, the portrait of his little-girl mamma was a neverfailing interest, and he often said—prompted doubtless by the recitals and romances of his nurse—that the argosy bore their better fortune, and would put about some day, in God's good time, and restore to them their missing treasure.

Ludovico, crossing the courtyard, noticed some one wrapped, like himself, in a silk cloak, coming from Isabelle's residence. He called; the figure halted, then advanced with bared head, and he recognized Bernardino Corte.

"What is here amiss?" exclaimed the duke,

angry and suspicious at the untimely presence of the governor, and still filled with the impressions of the anonymous warning.

"Merely a round of duty," replied Bernardino, with perfect assurance. "After visiting the posts I stopped to inquire of the lady within concerning a message the castellana brought me."

"Such evening visits will breed scandal; you will listen to her messages by daylight hereafter."

"Hereafter I shall leave them wholly to your pleasure, Signor Duca," replied the other, with an accent of sarcasm piercing the suavity of his voice.

Ludovico moved abruptly away, and, ascending the stair, whose arched walls were lighted by a single taper, entered Isabelle's room unannounced, and, pausing at the threshold, threw aside his cap and cloak, and took in at a glance the familiar aspect of the room and the group before him,—the sturdy boy with eyes intent, the mother in robes of mourning, and in her hair a band of gold, sole relic of her lost insignia. And in the pale statuesque face she turned toward him he read the first quick glance of aversion, that faded instantly to the bland composure of Italian self-restraint.

She rose as he entered and stood looking fixedly at him. Fastened about the waist of her bodice was a silver chain, to which were attached a pair of scissors, a crucifix, and a diminutive breviary, which she held in her hands before her. At her throat and wrists, and where the sleeves of her dress were slashed at the elbow, after the fashion of the time, was a border of linen; her hair curled over her brow and fell at her side in braids, and upon the back of her head was a small pointed cap with edging of lace.

"You will, pray, pardon my abrupt intrusion," began Sforza.

"I beg you to be seated," answered Isabelle, motioning coldly to a chair, and resuming her place.

The duke settled himself at his ease, nodded good-naturedly to the boy Francesco, and said in his quiet voice:

"You must sometimes be lonesome here, and for once, having matters of comforting and reassuring import to speak of, I have interrupted your quiet evening with glad tidings."

"I am ready to listen," replied the lady, with an indifference suggestive of small faith in the promised good news; then, addressing her child, who had dropped his porridge-spoon and sat leaning forward upon his elbows with his wondering gaze rivetted upon the duke, she said:

"Franceschino mio, get thee to bed: Maria waits in the room yonder; close fast the door, and omit not thy prayers."

"First bid me good-night," said Ludovico, holding out both hands to the boy, who had risen and kissed his mother. "How stout a youth we grow!" he continued, as the child drew reluctantly toward him. "Shake hands, so, felicissima notte, and listen, will you hear a word of good sense? When you are a man, gather information from all, but take advice from none. Can you remember that?"

"But some people take everything," objected the child.

"Bah!" ejaculated the duke, stung by the aptness of the retort, "at least they will not get thy good looks, nor the care-free heart that beats under thy jacket."

"To bed, to bed," interposed Isabelle, as the boy was about to answer; then, when the door closed, she added with a sudden and vehement bitterness:

"You come to taunt me as ever—to mock at the helpless fate of my child! Ah, may it be your punishment after death, since there is no retribution here on earth, to see your descendants make havoc with the fair fame and the riches and the power you have filched from me and mine."

"By heaven, you wrong me!" ejaculated Il Moro, starting from his easy position, and crossing himself with a look of superstitious alarm. "I come to speak kindly, and, however unwelcome myself, to tell you something you will be infinitely glad to hear."

"It were strange, indeed, to receive good tidings!" retorted the duchess, relapsing into an apathy of manner which had become habitual.

"First, are we alone? No eavesdroppers about your walls?"

"None: the old nurse is deaf, as you know."

"True, I forgot, no one comes here but myself."

"Then say on,—stay!" interposed Isabelle, with a woman's subtle perception; "when you say none come here, you mean, with the next breath, to accuse me of receiving Bernardino Corte, whom quite probably you met in the court."

"Has Bernardino been here?" asked Sforza, with a puzzled look. "What can possibly bring him to you at this hour?"

"How can I tell what brings him? Of course it is not the reason he gives, that you have bidden him torment me."

"I shall reprove him for meddling," answered the duke with an evident displeasure, which Isabelle rightly attributed to vexation at seeing his inquiry baffled. "And now," he continued, resuming the courtly manner that had left him in that moment's impatience, "to the matter that brings me. It is a month since I last spoke with you, and in four weeks many things have happened."

"It is to the next four weeks I chiefly look," observed Isabelle with malice that showed through the calm of her measured speech.

"Because you anticipate misfortune to me?

Were it not wiser to conciliate my advances than to buffet them back?"

The duke spoke with quick, spontaneous feeling, his figure bending forward, his arms extended.

Isabelle flushed in resentment at words that seemed so gross a perversion, and answered in a vehement burst of anger:

"I conciliate your advances!" she cried with scornful indignation, 'you, that sought to prevent my wedding!—that persecuted Galeazzo till he died broken-hearted, powerless to smite you save with the silent reproach of his eyes!—you, that have deprived me of all you now possess, that have kept me these years imprisoned, and fed me upon the griefs that every anniversary recalls!—you, whose interest it is to kill my child, and whose cruel heart bids you strike! Can such as you be the friend of the defenceless?"

Ludovico, listening with cold and dangerous anger glittering in his eyes, measured in that instant the full magnitude of his captive's desolation. Under the conflicting emotions aroused by her words he hesitated for an instant, and, turning from her, walked up and down the further end of the room, to pause at length before the little oratory. He looked with a curious interest at the altar, and at the cherubim frescoed on the wall, that had floated down a century with scarce diminished bloom of cheek, and with the same seraphic joy. At his feet rested a cradle of elaborate carving, which he eyed with a bitter smile. In it had been rocked, in infancy, four generations of Sforza, — the child Francesco, Galeazzo, Galeazzo Maria, and Francesco the elder. His thoughts passed from the boy who had gone to his rest in the adjoining room, to the sad life of that boy's father; to Galeazzo Maria and his career of storm and shadow; and back to the Francesco of a hundred years ago, who had founded their fortune and their name. And looking at this humble reminder of a sombre past, the impressions of the lowering present filled him with a sudden weariness of life; of its ingratitudes devoured in secret; of its false signposts that cheat discretion; of its chagrins decked out in harlequin's disguise. And moved by a sudden impulse, and softened by a tender remembrance, Ludovico walked quickly back to where Isabelle sat, and said:

"You do me injustice. The jealousies and rivalries with which you and my Beatrice afflicted one another impelled me beyond my deliberate intention."

"Spare me at least the mention of that hateful name."

"Speak not harshly of the dead; whatever has been done amiss is beyond remedy, nor would it avail me anything to excuse or defend the past. It is of the future I would speak of the future of yourself and your child. You are not unaware that a great danger threatens Milan?"

"You began by intimating as much," answered the ex-duchess, with a look of suppressed triumph.

"But you know more than I have told you," objected Il Moro, as his suspicion reverted to the governor's clandestine visit. "Said Bernardino Corte nothing?"

"Ay, he did; he said you were at war with France, and that your army is commanded by a certain Sanseverino, whom I myself remember as a captain of the parade ground—a feeble chief, methinks, to send in the face of an enemy?"

"And what said he more?"

"Nothing; but the populace must be making ready to rise against you, when the castellana said yesterday she had sent her children to a distance."

"They are babbling fools!" exclaimed Ludovico, disconcerted by these dexterous thrusts. "It matters not. They shall have small occasion for further confidence. It was to tell you great news that I came here to-night. I am about to set you and Francesco at liberty—you start—well, it is not wholly to me you owe this. I see in it my own advantage, since your release will divert much of the fury of this storm, at least so far as to appease the Milanese. Mark you with what openness I speak. But, further, your liberation has been asked by my nephew as the reward of an infinite service. If he acquit himself well, the Venetian advance will be stayed: your release averts the peril of an uprising within the city, and leaves me clear to meet the French with all my forces and with myself at their head; and therefore I have consented to Hermes' condition. Immediately upon his return, a troop of horse shall escort you southward to your beloved Bari, and you and I will distress one another no more."

Taught by evil experience, Isabelle scanned this project only to discover its ulterior motive. To her view, so suspicious a proffer must cover a snare. Moreover, she had in Bernardino Corte a secret and ambitious friend, whom, in the impending crisis, she meant to use to tremendous purpose. She knew that a withdrawal at this decisive moment meant the abandonment of the sovereignty she had never ceased to claim, and a far-reaching plan flashed upon her as she answered:

"You have kept me here against my will, and now that this prison has become my only refuge, you thrust me from it."

To this Ludovico replied with an impatience which confirmed the duchess in her ominous misgiving.

"Your release has been for years entreated by yourself and many others!" he exclaimed, "and now that it is granted you reject it?"

"In such perilous times I should surely run upon some misadventure; while here, as you and Bernardino Corte have sworn a thousand times, I need fear nothing."

"But," objected the duke, with a decided gesture, "times are changed since those assurances were given, and the day may come, ere long, when this citadel will be besieged,—when its garrison may have to endure extreme privation. How will you fare then?"

The duchess eyed him, as he spoke, with intense and deliberate scrutiny, and read, as she imagined, a world of dissimulation in his face. Then, with a laugh of sardonic incredulity, she answered:

"If, indeed, this fortress stands as the last bulwark of our family, then here, among its defenders, is my place."

Il Moro felt the irony of this reply, and with an angry imprecation he retorted:

"It is a necessity that you leave Milan, and you shall go, —if need be, strapped to the back of the horse that carries you!"

"Ah! now, at last, we touch the truth!" exclaimed Isabelle, with an outcry of pretended surprise and rage; "it is thus you grant me liberty, —to please Hermes, forsooth! I am to be carried away by force at the mercy of a band of your bravos, and, in some defile of the Apennines, a couple of sword-strokes will rid you of me and of Francesco forever."

"By St. Peter, Hermes shall prove the truth of my words."

"Good! Bring him here, and what Hermes tells me I will believe."

The duke's countenance suddenly changed.

"I cannot bring Hermes," he said. "He has left the castle and could not now be found; to-morrow at daybreak he leaves Milan."

"Could not now be found! Why, but an hour ago I saw him idling across the courtyard. Ah, Sforza, you know you dare not bring him face to face with me."

Perplexed by the taunts of this helpless woman, and stung by these successive affronts, the duke stood silent, and his face, that had reddened with anger, grew pale.

"Mark you that!" cried the duchess, with hand outstretched as though she would have smitten him, "a lie, 'tis said, brings a blush, and shame can blanch even the cheek of a tyrant."

The duke's eyes were fastened upon her in ominous silence, and his fingers closed upon the ready stiletto, but Isabelle heeded nothing.

"Torment me no longer with your proffers and regrets," she said, "nor seek to pass the gulf that separates us. Fare you back to your council chamber and order the march of your army; and when you lie awake in the silence of the dawn, you will hear, as I do, something in the air that bodes of great events. 'Twas but last night I dreamt that all my sorrows came to me with glistening eyes and radiant faces, each one of them transfigured. Oh! you may scoff and sneer, yet you should covet dreams like these, though you are free. What evil remembrances must come to you, what disquieting visions, what forebodings of the day when hostile cannon shall be trained upon these walls, and the French flag is carried in triumph through yonder streets."

Ere she finished speaking came a sound at which both started—a sharp and imperative rap at the knocker. It was an interruption of evidently serious import, and both paused for an instant and drew back from one another. Then the duke threw wide the door and beheld one of his own pages.

"What is it, boy?" he exclaimed eagerly, though with an accent of relief.

"Signor Duca, a despatch marked *Immediate;* Messer Bernardino bade me bring it here at once." And the youth presented a parchment double sealed and fresh from a courier's wallet.

Ludovico brought the letter to the light. The watchful Isabelle read its ill news in his overclouding brow, and caught the words he muttered above his breath:

"*Cremona taken by the Venetians!*"

He folded the letter, while his eyes instinctively sought the duchess. But Isabelle was no longer in the room. He looked about him and beheld her kneeling at the oratory altar, with her arms extended to heaven.

CHAPTER IV.

THE MARRIAGE OF THE SEA.

HERMES had little difficulty in persuading Narvaez to start with him on the following morning, in consideration of a purse of ducats, and upon the stipulation that he should serve merely as guide and companion, and be in no wise responsible for the discharge of their mission, which, though vaguely indicated, the fencing-master divined to be beyond his methods. As he had lived in Venice and knew the ways of the people, and could thread his way afoot through its labyrinths, his selection promised to be of more practical value than Ludovico had conceived it.

The first day of their journey was spent in one of the canvas-covered post-wagons of the period, which, passing by a northern route, brought them in rear of the Venetian army. Here they were made to exhibit their papers, and were delayed by the march of a rear guard of Stradiot light horse and Dalmatian infantry; here, too, they passed the provveditori, whose charge it was to watch the conduct of every general in the field; and not far behind came a company of leeches, nurses, and cooks, destined for the care of the wounded. Early on the third morning they entered a gondola, and glided swiftly across the lagoon of Fusina, leaving behind the fishing-boats, whose red sails waited vainly for the breeze, and the round-bowed market barges with freight of poultry and vegetables. Against the creamy flushes of the eastern sky appeared the pointed campanili, and above a misty outline of roofs rose domes and spires. Southward lay a sandbar which hid the sea, whose salt odor reached them; but toward the north they beheld successive lines of violet hills, and behind them the dolomites of Cadore and the peak of the giant Antelao. Narvaez directed their course to an obscure trattoria in the quarter called Il Rialto, which gave its name to a floating wooden bridge on the Grand Canal. They passed under many arched footways, nearly grazing the corners as they turned with musical splash of the oars. Hermes laughed with delight at the glimpses of marble balconies and colonnades, and of frescoes brilliant as flowers.

A sudden cry—Sciar!—and a backward dip, and they were before the slimy and discolored steps which gave ingress to the hiding-place which Narvaez had selected. Its first impression upon the fastidious Hermes was of an odor of seaweed and floating substances long past their prime; nor was this perception bettered by the information that the cheer of the house was so meagre as to have procured for it the nickname of l'Osteria della Fame, *the hungry hotel.*

"We shall pass our time here undisturbed," whispered the fencing-master, with unintended sarcasm, as they seated themselves alone in the eating-room, while the servants bustled away for breakfast.

"Think you I will eat or sleep beside a kitchen that gives out that musty odor?"

"But, signore mio, you bade me bring you to a place where even the Council of Ten—an ill digestion to them—could not find you, and you drop into this bird's nest and are as completely lost to sight as though your uncle's soothsayer had whisked you back to Milan."

"Well, well," answered Hermes impatiently, "let us eat and be gone; we will hasten to that famous piazzetta—the andata starts at three—perhaps we may leave Venice to-night."

An hour later they sallied out at the rear of the hungry hotel, and crossed the Rialto, where Hermes cast a wondering glance at the type of Shylock in Jewish gaberdine, and overheard more than one Bassanio chatting with his friends; and where, pausing to gaze down the vista of the Grand Canal, he saw young faces, gravely beautiful as Portia's, passing, as the gondolas— brilliant in those days with gilding and polished woods and varied colors—flew noiselessly by.

"How is it," exclaimed Hermes, looking about him, " that you lived a year in this place and never talked to me of it?"

"I once began to tell you of the piazzetta," replied the Spaniard. "I said that great diamonds sparkling made me think of Venice—and at that you laughed, and I said no more."

They passed on through a street which widened around a well with its stone rim grooved where the ropes had been lowered and raised for centuries, until they reached the Merceria, or arcade of shops, with its profusion of wares—filigree, mirrors, mosaics, silks and velvets, spices and tapestries, ivory and weapons, indulgences from Rome, and relics from the Holy Land. Through the clock tower they emerged upon the Piazza San Marco, and, for a moment, both paused to gaze upon the scene thus disclosed.

The great fair annually held at the feast of the Marriage of the Sea was nearly over, in consequence of this year's postponement of the festival; but the piazza was still surrounded by a row of temporary shops, while of the thousands who resorted to Venice in the spring-time of every year, enough still lingered to fill the square with gay and busy groups. Before St. Mark's stood three flagstaffs, from which floated the gonfalons em-

blematic of the chief dominions of the republic,
Candia, Cyprus, and the Morea. Beyond rose the
two immortal red pillars and the carnation façade
of the doge's palace; before it troops of children
went hither and thither, strewing flowers in imitation of a festival of the Levant called the Scattering of the Roses, while in the shade of the promenade of the Broglio—whose name, "*the Brawl*,"
suggests the noisy conversation of the ancient
Venetians sat the Italian story-teller unfolding
his exhaustless romance to knots of dreamy listeners, who from time to time sipped coffee and
oriental sherbets.

On the broad expanse of water before them the
sunlight laid its radiant gleams,—a reflex, thought
Hermes, of that brilliant tracery with which Venice
has written her incomparable story upon the sea.
In the foreground several vessels rode at anchor,—
argosies with half-spread sails, and close together
a Spanish felucca and an English two-master,
whose crews exchanged disparaging repartees,—
while off the marble steps lay the doge's renowned
galley, *Il Bucentoro*: its gilded surface, the multitude of polished oars folded against its sides, the
costly draperies which shaded its decks, and the
immense lanterns and flags with which it was decorated, giving it an appearance in keeping with the
mystical grandeur of the ceremony to which it was
chiefly dedicated.

"How can I hope to be admitted?" murmured Hermes, "still less to conceal myself on board?"

"That you may get on board," answered the Spaniard, "is not impossible; but that you should be permitted to approach the doge seems preposterous. But our first care should be to reconnoitre, as it were, the enemy's stronghold; for this we need a boat."

"But," objected Hermes, "to employ Venetian boatmen would be to put a guard upon ourselves."

"I have foreseen that," replied Narvaez, motioning away the men who, observing their scrutiny of the quay, pressed forward like hungry animals, with cries of "*gondole, gondole.*" Then, leading his companion toward the quarter frequented by foreign sailors, he added: "And for that reason are we to meet here on the Riva de' Schiavoni a couple of trusty lads whom the hotel has provided—a brace of Spaniards I asked for—stay, that fellow with patched breeches, see, he comes towards us."

"Have I ever seen you before?" inquired Narvaez softly, as the boatman approached.

"*Osteria della Fame*, yes," answered the sailor, speaking with a Maltese accent.

"Have you a boat?"

"Not I, signore; do you take me for a wealthy nobleman like yourself?"

"There were to be two men and a pinnace."

"Misericordia! and is not everything prepared?

—all thanks to St. Michael! My mate is a Greek, a God-fearing man, and yonder lies his boat."

"Call me your Greek and make ready."

The Maltese returned with a sailor roughly clad as himself, and with the ignoble face and fawning speech of the modern Hellene.

"Will foreign boatmen like yourselves be allowed to follow the andata?"

"We will not follow, we will precede it," replied the Greek, with a cunning smile; "besides, it is a public festival, whoever will may go."

"Aboard, then, and look to it that we infringe no rule of the port or of the master of ceremonies; and first steer to the Bucentoro, that we may view her closer."

They hoisted sail and pointed towards the doge's galley. Already, at this early hour, it seemed a hive of beings; on the deck were gathered senators and nobles, the ambassadors of foreign states, and ladies of rank; near the prow the Papal nuncio conversed with half a dozen monsignori; a throng of musicians with the famous silver trumpets stood at the stern, while below deck could be heard the bustling and talking of the hundreds of slaves who were presently to pull at the oars.

"My uncle's command is folly," whispered Hermes with vexation; "there is no sense in even following the andata."

"Nevertheless, illustrissimo, lose not the chance

of this occasion; the eyes of all will be so engrossed that every soul will presently be heedless of what is done apart this ceremonial."

"Be it so," murmured Hermes resignedly; "if I am not at the andata, Ludovico will say I missed the opportunity; it will prove useless, and to-night we will seek the doge at his palace."

This consultation had been hurriedly carried on in an undertone, apparently unnoticed by the Maltese, who handled the ropes at the bow, or by the Greek who held the tiller. Obedient to a further order they now steered towards a shoal of islands to the eastward, and presently reached the tranquil sea outside the Lido, whither a number of sailboats and gondolas were similarly going. They continued as far as the outer limit of the Porto del Lido, where the celebration was to be performed, when the Greek interrupted their desultory talk with an exclamation, and, pointing back, indicated a large vessel, which, propelled both by oars and sails, was already half way from shore, with a queue of small boats in its wake.

"That is not the Bucentoro," objected Narvaez.

"No, master," replied the Greek; "it is the galley of the anti-doge, filled with buffoons and jugglers and some hundreds of merry fellows, and they make all manner of sport with their dancing and antics and songs, and at last they wed the sea with a barrel-hoop."

As he ceased speaking, they heard the salutes fired that announced, as far as the sound could reach, the sailing of the sacred Bucentoro.

The anti-doge drew near to where the small boats clustered together, and the exuberance of the light-hearted populace filled the air with jibes and shouts. But ere long all eyes were fixed upon the sailless ship, which, rounding the point with its myriad oars, came swiftly towards them, till presently they could distinguish the brilliant throng that covered its deck, and, as the multitude of boats made way, a loud command was given and the oars were held together in the foaming water. The shouts on the harlequin's galley ceased, the talk of the occupants of a multitude of gondolas was hushed, and the few that had remained behind came hurrying after; and in the crowding that followed the pinnace was left astern.

There was an interval of waiting till all was quiet. Then, amid the impressive silence that reigned over the assembled thousands, and with every face intent upon him, the Primate of Venice arose and stood at the prow between the banner of St. Mark and the white standard of the Sovereign Pontiff, and prayed. He asked that the ashes of St. Mark might be more and more honored, that the enemies of Venice might be confounded, that the emblematic nuptials about to be performed might, in very truth, be typical of substantial and enduring supremacy. And while his arms were stretched above the placid Adriatic, and his rich, vibrating voice was lifted to heaven, Narvaez, glancing at the stern of the Bucentoro, whispered to his companion:

"Through one of those open windows the galley might be boarded; not an eye but is fixed upon her prow."

"My life would pay for it," muttered Hermes; "it were suicide to risk so wild a cast."

"You never made a wiser resolve," replied the Spaniard, as with a relieved expression he bade the boatman push forward.

The prayer had ended, and in place of the robust person of the primate there advanced a venerable man with snowy beard and thin, sunken face and high brow, and on his head the ducal beretta, and about him an embroidered garment that fell to his feet. And standing beneath the traditional crimson umbrella, famous as the gift of a Pope, he gazed upon the thousands of upturned faces, upon the brightly painted gondolas with draperies and jewelled slaves, and then, beyond, upon his shining and beautiful bride, and in a half audible voice he invoked the blessing of Heaven upon Venice, and with a gesture of loving and reverent salutation pronounced in Latin the words: "We wed thee, O Sea, in token of true and everlasting sovereignty," —and threw far forward the sanctified ring which should rivet these strange nuptials, and which fell sparkling with a slight splash into the water.

And now arose an outcry of voices that drowned for a moment the burst of music which smote the air with martial strains. The gondolas opened a way for the Bucentoro, which resumed its onward course, and, describing a half circle, headed in the direction of the church of San Niccolò, where the doge was to hear mass.

As they returned to the landing whence they had put forth, "There must be," said Hermes, "some dainty cookshop hereabouts where we can rest and sup; I am athirst and hungry and jaded."

"Half a dozen such are on the piazza."

"Then dismiss these villainous boatmen and let us have a luxurious repast. With a fiasco of good wine, I shall talk to-night as impressively as the primate himself. For, look you, Narvaez, I dare not trust myself and you and the letters all at once in the doge's presence. We might be intercepted, and then all were lost. And so I shall leave the letters with you; here, button them securely within your doublet, and you shall wait without while I gain a hearing, and if all is well they shall be delivered: otherwise, if aught befall me, you shall use them to-morrow to effect my release."

Arrived at the red pillars, Hermes observed a trattoria whose appearance satisfied him. As they neared it, Narvaez said:

"Since you have so strong an aversion for the hotel to which I conducted you, I have thought of another this side the Grand Canal, where we shall fare better with nearly equal concealment, and to which, while you order, I will have the saddle-bags removed."

"Can you be back within half an hour?"

"Yes, for it is but a step from here."

Half an hour had elapsed, and the stars were beginning to twinkle, when Narvaez returned to the piazza, where he found the crowd as animated as in the morning, and more noisy. Before the eating-shop at which he had left Hermes were ranged tables al fresco, but the Spaniard searched for him in vain. He glanced over the fantastic scene,— the façade of St. Mark's, lighted with fairy tracery by the lanterns before it; the hundreds of lights which flared and flickered in the wind above the tables of the venders; the odd costumes from far countries; the chattering puppet-shows in which Italians delight. Then he grew troubled at the thought that something amiss must have befallen, —and now his quick ear was fixed upon the talk of a group, whose words explained this disappearance.

"I stand to it," said one, "the fellows are madmen: who else would think to board the Bucentoro? Who else would trust themselves and their plot to a couple of gondoliers?"

"No," objected a second, "it is clear enough; the Greek knew them by their speech to be Milanese; it is a resort of Duke Sforza to suspend the war by assassinating the doge."

"What a pity only one of them was taken!" remarked a third, "but his mate will be found before morning."

"He was a cool rascal," laughed the one who had first spoken, "to regale himself on the public piazza between his attempts on Barbarigo. How queerly he looked when his boatmen came with the signori di notte!"

At these words Narvaez turned away instinctively, and, skirting the piazza, buried himself in the first alley. Arrived at the deep arch of a closed door, he halted.

"A sleeveless errand, this!" he muttered with an imprecation: "my only hope is to reach the doge. I know where he lives—I will go afoot—no more boatmen for me."

It was no great distance to the Palazzo Barbarigo. Narvaez threaded his way through narrow and tortuous streets, often crossing the bridges which enable those familiar with the city to reach any quarter. More than once he paused to read the name beneath the lanterns placed at great intervals. Arrived at his destination, a summons with the knocker brought a black slave to the peephole, through which he reconnoitred the stranger, while demanding his business in the coarse Italian peculiar to the Moors. Ludovico's letter to the doge's brother was delivered, and presently the younger Barbarigo appeared. He evidently regarded Narvaez with misgiving; but the nature of his introduction from a prince and a friend, albeit an enemy, secured him an audience, after conforming to the usual etiquette of laying aside his stiletto.

Seated in a luxurious arm-chair at the extremity of a large room sat Barbarigo, habited in skull-cap, cashmere vest, and easy gown. Behind him had been stationed two Slavonian guards, each leaning upon a weapon of formidable aspect. The younger Barbarigo, who was his brother's secretary, followed Narvaez, and placed himself beside the old man's chair.

"They take me for a spadaccino!" was the fencer's thought as he bowed reverently and remained standing and silent.

The doge turned to his brother and said querulously, "Ask what brings him here to vex us, and by what chance he is possessed of a letter from Il Moro?"

"You hear the question," said the secretary, speaking with the decided utterance of one accustomed to authority. "Answer, and raise your voice—the doge's hearing is imperfect."

Thus summoned, the Spaniard, with some trepidation, made reply. "Your serenity," he began, "I came from Milan as the companion of Hermes Sforza, nephew to the duke, who was entrusted with a weighty and confidential mission, and who would be here with me to declare his business in proper terms were it not that a strange mishap has befallen him."

"Tell him to speak louder," interrupted Barbarigo, leaning forward, "and to come briefly to his wish."

"That, my masters," resumed Narvaez, "could only be set forth by Sforza, and my present purpose is simply to entreat that he may be restored to liberty and permitted to speak his message."

"Where, then, is your companion?" inquired the secretary, perceiving that Barbarigo was at a loss to make much of this confused declaration.

"Alas!" exclaimed Narvaez, divining the awkward impression he was making, "it is beyond my power to tell more than that I believe him to have been seized, an hour ago, by the signori di notte."

"The signori di notte do not arrest for nothing; he must have made some disturbance—a street brawl, eh?"

"I left him on the piazza, and, when I came again, he was gone; but the talk of some people near by revealed that in my absence we had been denounced by a pair of boatmen we employed to-day, and that he had been carried off."

"Denounced!" ejaculated Barbarigo, who caught a fragment here and there. "For what were you denounced?"

"Upon some mistake of the boatmen, who attributed to us a sinister motive of which we are innocent, and which it is therefore difficult to define."

"This is a strangely halting story," remarked the secretary, "and you are keeping back that which is essential to make it intelligible. Answer my questions, and withhold aught at your peril. When did you arrive in Venice?"

"This morning."

"If you came from Milan, how did you pass the lines of the Venetian army?"

"As honest citizens travelling upon business, and furnished with the usual safe-conduct."

"A safe-conduct in time of war? That equals the wild statement, with which you began, about a message from the Duke of Milan."

"Yes, given to his nephew, who brought me with him."

"What is your profession?"

At this question Narvaez recovered the self-possession which was fast deserting him, and, smiling complacently, replied, "Master of the rapier, and instructor in the use of the main gauche, the stiletto, the——"

"Per l'Ostia! a spadaccino. And what is this

mysterious accusation upon which your comrade was arrested?"

"Signore," answered the fencer, wincing at the return to this delicate point, "it is impossible to explain what I know not; but, I beseech you, bring him hither and let him answer for himself."

"I have a greater mind to send you to join him at the pozzi!" broke in the doge, who had followed this interrogatory.

"We both came in all honor, as under a flag of truce."

The younger Barbarigo motioned his brother to restrain his impatience; then his face darkened ominously. "You talk lightly of this harlequinade," he began, in a voice of menacing harshness, "as a secret embassy from Sforza with whom we are at war; know you not that if this purpose is declared to-morrow, such a messenger would be accounted a spy?"

"Eccellenza, you need but say a word to spare him from examination."

"What! Shield a man whose act is treason to Venice? You shall be taught to understand us better. Mark me! You came possessed of a letter which entitled you to a hearing, in the course of which you acknowledge yourself to be a professional bravo, and the escort of one we must not receive or listen to if you have interpreted his mission aright. Upon an accusation which is not explained, and which does not weigh in your favor, he is seized by the guard. If to-morrow he but breathe the purpose you attribute to him, he will be arraigned before the council as a spy; and that you should seek to move the doge to connive at this criminal mission is your last and greatest offence. I shall now have you taken to the signori di notte, and, whatever befalls, we, at least, will stand blameless."

The stout-hearted Narvaez felt his courage sink at this startling metamorphosis of their position, and, as the last words were uttered, he threw himself at the feet of the secretary, and extended the second letter, which Hermes should have delivered in person to the doge.

"Another missive!" cried the younger Barbarigo angrily.

"It explains all. In the name of the innocent, read it; but as you dread the powers to which you would commit us, read it alone."

"We *are* alone," replied the secretary curtly: "these Slavs comprehend nothing." Then, taking the letter, he drew a chair to the side of his brother, who bent forward with an old man's eagerness as the parchment was opened.

Their eyes rested upon it together, and at the first glance the doge's face contracted with a sudden spasm, and he raised a startled and affrighted gaze upon the Spaniard; his brother read down the paper, then crumpled it violently in his hands, and, rising with a ghastly face from the seat he had just taken, cast a furtive look about the room to assure himself that no other eye had beheld the writing.

Narvaez observed with stupor the effect of this second letter, but the secretary left him little time for wonder.

"Do you know what is here written?" he asked, in a subdued and altered voice.

"No," answered the Spaniard, with a bluntness that carried conviction.

"And Sforza — ?"

"Told me he received it sealed from the hand of his uncle."

The secretary breathed a sigh of relief, smiled reassuringly at his brother, and held the letter in the flame of a lamp till its last vestige curled in cinders; these he bore to the nearest window and dropped into the canal.

He returned to the side of the doge, and they conversed in an idiom of Greek used among Venetian merchants. Presently the younger Barbarigo addressed Narvaez with a kindliness that brought the fencer a fresh surprise.

"So particular a letter from our brother of Milan," he said, "commands us; to-morrow morning young Sforza shall be freed and shall tell his message. Fear nothing; but, that you may meet with no further mishap, you shall pass this night in an antechamber, to which you will now be conducted. And take this caution: should you have so foolish a thought as to wish to leave our roof by stealth, act not upon it as you value life."

CHAPTER V.

THE STAR CHAMBER.

On the following morning Narvaez was awakened from an uneasy slumber by the ringing of the Angelus, which all the bells in Venice took up, each with its own peculiar voice, from the deep, loud stroke of the clock tower, and the musical clangor of church campanili, to the tuneful and tinkling cadence of cloister chimes. In the fancy of the sleeping youth their distant and softened pealing recalled the familiar cow-bells of his native sierras, and in his last moment of dreamy unconsciousness he beheld again the long lines of cattle trooping at dawn through the forest calm, and winding away to upland pastures amid the amethyst peaks.

He rose from an improvised couch with spirits depressed, and with a premonition that his misadventure was far from ended. He was presently visited by the chaplain of the house, who, after suavely reminding him that a meditation upon the beatitudes was the proper employment of the moments following his awakening, added that the doge was about to leave for the official palace, whither an escort should presently conduct him.

Half an hour later he was led to a gondola, which was swiftly directed down the Grand Canal, amid the animation and magnificence of the graceful palaces which stood in a continuous line of elaborately chiselled colonnades and balconies and pilasters and heavily-barred windows, and here and there, high on the wall, a diminutive Madonna. Tied to rusty piers lay pleasure-boats of gaudy coloring, and through open doorways could be seen a cortile with plants and vines of luminous green, or a cool, dim hallway with great white stairs, and statues, and arched mosaic roof. But Narvaez, in his dejection, scarce cast a glance upon them all, and it was with a feeling of impatient relief that he came within hearing of the bustle of the piazzetta, and landed on the steps of the private entrance to the doge's palace.

At the close of the fifteenth century the republic of Venice had attained its greatest development of genius and strength. In the religious fervor which, of old, tempered and enhanced so many virtues, its people kept the pristine faith; in the previous century it had dealt Genoa, its potent rival, a blow from which that commonwealth never recovered; the forces by land and sea were still of the heroic fibre of past generations, whose ultimate and final prowess, seventy years later, was to smite the Turkish armada at Lepanto; its commerce had not yet suffered by the Portuguese discovery of the Cape route to the Indies; its government was the most concentrated, the best informed, and the most cruel of the middle ages.

The administration of this redoubtable state was absorbed by a Senate representing the families inscribed upon the Libro d'Oro; since the failure of Faliero's plot to recover by bloodshed the prerogatives withdrawn piecemeal from the doge, the power of the nominal chief of the state had been further reduced, till now little remained but the exercise of high ceremonies, and the chair of honor in the great Council. But the Senate, in its turn, had suffered an equal encroachment from the Executive Council of Ten, and from the famous Council of Three, which held absolute power over life and property. It was before the second of these that Hermes was now to appear.

The fencing-master was led from the private landing through the central court, with its flights of sculptured stairs, and the domes and pinnacles of St. Mark's, and a profusion of palm trees and odorous shrubs, in imitation of the shaded and fragrant courts of Stamboul, and thence to a secluded room where sat Barbarigo and his brother. At sight of them the Spaniard rejoiced to know that they shared his predicament and would be glad as himself to shorten it. Motioning him to approach, and bidding his escort retire, Barbarigo addressed him in the suppressed tone to which a deaf man moderates his voice.

"Your companion," he began, "will presently be brought before me; a charge of conspiracy has been preferred against him. Tell me, had he other documents beside the two you brought?"

"Yes," answered Narvaez, hoping that the worse the case appeared the sooner it would be the doge's desire to end it; "only yesterday morning I saw him draw a roll of papers from his wallet."

"Have you knowledge of their import?" muttered Barbarigo, glancing nervously at his brother.

"There was a safe-conduct to pass the Venetian lines, some bills of exchange, and a map with notes of the way."

"By whom was the safe-conduct signed?"

"It looked regular enough, but the signature was fictitious."

"And the bills of exchange?"

"To say truth, they were imaginary also, being merely part of our equipment, so to speak, and intended, if we fell in with the Venetian troops, to bear us out in our character of clerks commissioned with some banker's business."

"And when this nephew of Sforza is examined, what story will he tell?"

"That we are entrusted with the sale of the exchanges he bears."

"Entrusted with the sale of forged bills, and travelling under a false safe-conduct! Those damning papers found upon him, and so lame a story on his tongue, he will be put to the question, and then——"

A light tap was heard at the door, and a confidential secretary entered and gravely said: "The young man is without, and the intendant of the prison craves, in addition to your order, a line declaring that the prisoner has been delivered to you."

"Said I not there must be no writing in this matter?" harshly answered Barbarigo; "that even my order for his release must be returned!"

"But the jailer dare not; remember he is accountable, and an accusation stands against the prisoner which——"

"Hush thy heedless tongue!" interrupted the doge's brother, with a meaning gesture towards the listening Narvaez. "Give him what he will, Barbarigo, we have no room now to hesitate."

The doge sullenly wrote the required receipt, and immediately Hermes entered the room, and the door behind him closed. Whatever satisfaction he may have felt at sight of his companion, or whatever greetings may have been upon his lips, all vanished before the words now addressed him.

"Young man," quoth the doge, with voice subdued by emotion, and with every perception intent, "you stand before me in grievous peril. I am heartily sorry for it, since imprudence is less to be blamed upon you than upon my brother of Milan. I would gladly set you free, but it is too late,—you will presently be required from me by an authority superior to mine. Profit by this moment, then, to tell me the words you bear from Sforza."

"Your Highness well knows," began Hermes, with earnestness, "the straits in which we of Milan stand through the double invasion we have to confront. To so painful a pass are we brought, that death were no worse than the shame which must presently overwhelm us. Our army can face the French, for, however outnumbered, we have stout hearts and strong walls, and time saves many a beleaguered army. But therein lies the limit of our resistance. If the soldiers of Venice unite with those of France, we shall utterly perish. Therefore, in the name of Sforza, I beseech you refrain from doing us so grievous a hurt. Suffer a generous compassion at the calamities that beset one whom a year ago you called friend to move you, and give us that respite which a brave man accords to the antagonist he sees overborne; halt your troops, delay their march for two months, set them to plundering our cities if you will; but, as you honor the reputation of Italian arms, grant that when we face the French it be not as men who fight without hope."

These were straightforward words, and they pierced to the sensibility of both the brothers.

"Woe is me," answered the doge, with veritable concern, "that I cannot do what you ask and what my desire would accord. But you know not Venice; the trouble of her neighbors has always been her opportunity—and is so now. The army has crossed your frontier; the provveditori watch the generals with jealous vigilance; what, then, can I, old, infirm, unable to leave this city, do to prevent their advance?"

"My uncle said, '*that which the righteous man steadfastly wills, the devil shall not prevent:*' moreover, he wrote a certain letter—Narvaez, I gave it you——"

"Ay, truly," interposed the doge; "it was faithfully delivered me last night." Then, after laboring with a spasm that took him as often as that cipher letter was mentioned, he went on to say: "You may tell the Duke of Milan that, as I am a Christian, I will seek to halt the troops, even to the limit of risking my life in the attempt. Tell me further," he added, "of your other papers—were they taken from you?"

"Yes, everything upon me, permit, bills of exchange, purse, jewels, everything, for they searched me from head to foot."

"And were you identified?"

"Yes, by two rogues of boatmen."

"No matter, all can be remedied, and all shall yet be well, provided you leave everything implicitly to my judgment."

Hermes was about to assent to this reassuring declaration, when an imperative summons was heard. Barbarigo's eyes fell at the sound, and his fingers trembled as they toyed with a long quill pen. Then, with abrupt resolution, he spoke as one who nerves himself for an excruciating ordeal.

"Hermes Sforza," he said, "this is a message from the Council; we must not be found so many. Withdraw with my brother into the adjoining room, and confer with him upon the best means of departure. And you, good youth," he pursued, addressing Narvaez, "wait here; I have some special direction to give you as to the part that you shall play,—draw near to me, so; when the door opens you must be found standing thus, receiving my command."

Hermes looked askance at this separation, but the knocking was loudly renewed, and Barbarigo's brother caught him by the arm, and whispering, "For all our sakes, *come!*" drew him away, and, having bolted the door, leaned his back against it.

And now the doge, being left alone with Narvaez, bade whoso knocked enter, and instantly there appeared a messenger, who saluted Barbarigo with reverence, though, with malicious intention, leaving ajar the door, so that an officer and six halberdiers could be seen standing in the hall.

"What business brings you thus impetuously?" asked the doge, with an abruptness of tone and an aversion of manner he did not attempt to conceal.

"I am ordered by the clerk of the Council to ask the reason for which you, this morning, ordered the release of a prisoner named Hermes Sforza, accused of high treason, and to require his instant attendance."

"My proceeding will not fail to commend itself. That an unknown youth, and a stranger, should harbor designs against my life, seemed so incomprehensible that, for my own honest information, I wished to question him in gentleness before he should pass to the sterner ordeal of the Inquisitors."

"It shall be so answered: now bid him follow me."

"One moment is needed to finish the inquiry you broke in upon, and by my faith it shall last no longer. What, man! think you I would release him, or fear you he can escape?"

The messenger yielded with ill grace, muttering as he withdrew.

When the doge turned from this colloquy, he perceived by the change in the bright young face that the sacrifice about to be required had been guessed. Barbarigo rose from his seat, caught

Narvaez by the hand, and whispered: "You must go; you must take the place of Hermes Sforza. It seems to you a fearful thing, but so it must be. Bear a bold heart; fear not but I will work to save you as though you were my own flesh and blood."

"Why must I take Hermes' place?" asked Narvaez, whose lips quivered as he spoke.

"Because there is a terrible risk about that which otherwise awaits him—perhaps the question, possibly worse—see, I conceal nothing from you."

"But, again I ask, why put me in his place?"

"Because the devil's letter you thrust in my hand last night binds me to the Duke of Milan by an obligation I shudder to recall. It were an ill beginning, since I am to serve him, to let his nephew be done to death. You alone now can take the risk; you can pass for Sforza, for you will appear only before the Council and their attendants, not one of whom has seen him. Make the best defence you can, and trust to me to secure your escape to-night."

"And Hermes?"

"Shall be out of Venice before the sun touches the horizon."

The young swordsman listened with a flush of color that died suddenly away; then, with an accent of determination beyond his years, he resolutely answered: "Be it as you will, and if I perish—let it be said to Hermes that I met this danger willingly to save him."

Meanwhile Hermes eagerly availed himself of his opportunity to question the doge's brother upon the events of the previous night, and that personage was soon volubly discoursing and gesticulating. The minutes passed; the hall door of the doge's room was repeatedly opened and closed; at length all was quiet. Their desultory talk drew to an end; the secretary, still leaning against the door of communication, became silent.

"Narvaez is again alone with the doge," observed Hermes, after a listening pause; "let us to him,—our task is accomplished; we would haste from Venice."

The Venetian yielded to this importunity; he unbolted the door, and allowed Hermes to reënter the study, where, to his astonishment, he perceived Barbarigo alone.

He glanced about the room abruptly; then, with an angry face, he stammered: "The youth whom we left here with you—what has become of him?"

Barbarigo looked up with a troubled air, and hesitatingly answered: "The youth is gone—fear not—he shall return unharmed; it was the only recourse to spare you an examination."

"What! he has been taken before the Council!"

"The jailers came for their prisoner, and at my suggestion he consented to take your place."

At this hearing Hermes dashed his cap upon the ground with an oath, his face became purple with rage, and, turning upon the secretary, he made as though he would have taken that worthy by the throat.

"Would to Heaven you had asked me!" he ejaculated: "how quickly should I have refused it! But at least," he continued, smiting his hands passionately together, "give me some promise of his safety; tell me what this examination is to be, and when he will be released?"

Barbarigo wiped his face with a silk handkerchief; the midsummer sun was gaining power, and his emotions rendered him an uncomfortable prince. He murmured slowly, softly, though audibly to those about him, these singular words: "May my merciful Father above account this part of the expiation of the folly of my presumptuous youth." Then, raising his voice, he replied: "Your companion stands in no greater risk than I do in this solemn hour. It was my first duty to the Duke of Milan to rescue his nephew; it remained unavoidable that some one must take his place before the Council."

"But, in the fiend's name, why not blurt the truth and tell how trivial was our errand?"

"Trivial! Your purpose was a crime which Venice punishes with death."

"And if your Council find Narvaez guilty?"

"Then a means shall be found to save him."

"If his life be forfeit through fault of yours," answered Hermes, "I will make public everything that I have seen and heard in Venice, and hereafter, at the judgment day, I will cry vengeance upon you!"

"Peace, poor fool," answered Barbarigo, "think you I could not in the next hour have your life taken, and leave your swordsman to his fate!"

"Say no more," whispered Barbarigo's brother to Hermes; "you may put faith in the doge, for he shares your peril in what has become a state secret; let us be silent now, and devote ourselves to your companion's rescue; and for you, meanwhile, a place of safety under this very roof has been contrived, where you shall receive frequent information and be in readiness for flight to-morrow. Follow me, then, by this private door; let us lose no time; come, let us go."

It was an ordinary circumstance for the members of the Council of Three to be summoned from rest, or pleasure, or private affairs, to sit, either as the Supreme Executive of the State, or as a court having the functions of judge, jury, and prosecutor. The news of a conspiracy had been conveyed to each during the night, and, upon first assembling, they had passed an hour in hearing read the record of the prisoner's examination upon his arrest, and in listening to the testimony of the boatmen. They had now finished with the report of the signori di notte; and the boatmen, having told their story, had been discharged: it was not the practice of the time, nor of that court, to put the prisoner in presence of his accusers, or of witnesses.

The three councillors sat at a table whereon stood an ivory crucifix. Writing at a high desk was their clerk, and leaning indifferently near a rack, whose fearful shape occupied one side of the room, was an African slave; in his hand he held a metal ball, with whose peculiar construction he toyed with the interest of one who examines a novel and ingenious mechanism; it was, in fact, a gag of improved workmanship, which, being thrust into the mouth of the person about to undergo the question, was, by the turn of a key, made to unfold to triple its size, thereby holding the sufferer's jaws distended and preventing an outcry. Before a window was a large arm-chair, above which, at a proper elevation, was firmly braced the celebrated helmet, which was the invention of Venice for summary execution. In it the head of the condemned was encased, and, at a signal, a turn of a wrench drove a long, sharp bolt deep into the base of the brain, severing the spinal column, and causing instantaneous death.

The three councillors, their clerk, and the negro looked up with a curious interest as the prisoner was conducted before them. They wondered what manner of man this reckless cut-throat the witnesses described would be, and all felt surprise at the delicate form and startled face of the youth who advanced with difficulty before them, his ankles being chained with a short fetter. His conductor scrupulously led him to a spot precisely in the centre of the room, placed his cap in his bound hands, and withdrew, closing the door, which the slave bolted.

If Narvaez had not at first comprehended the imminence and extremity of the danger he accepted, he realized it now in standing before a tribunal distinguished for never leaning to the side of mercy. He knew that to confess was to incur immediate sentence of death, with no hope beyond Barbarigo's frail promise of rescue. To deny was to be ordered instantly upon the rack. He looked at the judges before him in their scarlet robes, and read an unflinching purpose upon the face of each; then he glanced at the secretary, trimming his pens, and at the slave still fingering his metal gag; then his eye rested upon the rack, and at sight of that appalling instrument the anguish of despair came over him in a thought of convulsed lips, and starting eyes, and lacerated flesh, and sobs and shrieks.

"Young man," began the elder and apparently the chief of the Three, after a pause of silent scrutiny, "you come before us charged with the greatest offence known to the law of Venice. We are here to determine your punishment, and although the testimony setting forth your words and actions yesterday, corroborated by the forged and fictitious papers found upon you, leaves no doubt of your guilty purpose, yet such is the justice that rules the community against which you meditated a monstrous crime, that you shall not be deprived of a hearing nor of a single form of law. But that you may know how vain were any pretence of equivocation, you shall hear read the declarations which sustain the charge against you."

The unhappy Narvaez listened in a horrible bewilderment to the formal accusation, followed by the testimony of the two boatmen.

Once more his judge addressed him: "Do you acknowledge yourself to be the person charged with this plot?" he asked.

"Yes; I am Hermes Sforza, nephew to the Duke of Milan."

"And do you confess yourself guilty of the purpose to murder a harmless and defenceless old man?"

"What avails it to attempt a denial?" replied the prisoner.

"A denial!" echoed the Venetian; "nay, attempt it not. Beware how you tax our forbearance with denials. Only the full truth can mitigate, in some slight degree, the measure of your deserts. You admit, then, your guilt?"

It was only the choice between the immediate mutilation of the rack, and the supreme penalty, and Narvaez realized that he signed his own death-warrant in answering, "I do."

"But," pursued his examiner, "last evening, before the signori di notte, and in presence of the witnesses, you strenuously asserted innocence."

"I knew not then that the proof was conclusive against me."

"Perverted wretch! And what led you to such devilish malevolence?"

"The hope of saving Milan."

"You were not alone; your denouncers say you had a companion. Who was he?"

"A Spanish fencing-master named Narvaez."

The three councillors exchanged significant glances. Then the elder proceeded: "It is fortunate that you now repair your fault before the police in refusing to give his name; to show how futile was your boyish attempt to shield him, know that the osteria where you breakfasted was readily discovered, and that, by searching your luggage, enough was learned to establish the identity of you both. But one point remains, and I caution you to beware of any subterfuge. Where is this fellow concealed?"

"Has he not been taken?" exclaimed Narvaez.

"Answer me not with a question," replied the judge severely, "and hesitate at your peril."

"I last saw him yesterday, at sunset, on the piazza; before his return I was seized and carried off. If he were not found at the osteria, he must have fled from Venice on hearing of my arrest."

"It is impossible for him to have passed the guards; tell me instantly the familiar haunts in which he may have sought hiding, or you shall speak upon the rack."

"O masters!" answered Narvaez, with a despairing wail, "dispose of me as you will; to every question I have spoken the truth, and, however you may mutilate my poor body, upon this matter I shall still know only that I was twelve hours in Venice; that we went to but one public house; that the commonest thoroughfare in your city is unfamiliar to me; that it is impossible for me to know whither this youth may have betaken himself."

The inexorable face of the Venetian darkened with the sullen displeasure of one whose will brooks no denial. He turned to the expectant slave, and motioned a command which the latter awaited. He stepped to Narvaez, grasped him by the shoulders, and pushed him to the rack.

At this moment the councillor who sat at the left of him who had conducted the interrogatory, and who had more than once shown impatience at the elaboration with which obvious conclusions were reached, interposed. He had been summoned in the gray of the morning from the bedside of his dying child, and even the adamant of his spirit could be so far impressed as to abridge details and hang the accused with a short halter.

"What avails it," he exclaimed, "that we listen for the next hour to the whimpering of this harebrained boy? He cannot know where another rogue has run to, or, if he does, put him to something more intense than the rack—let him suffer the question in the first degree, and in five minutes we will have the truth and his vitals out together."

The slave paused, and the three Venetians engaged in a brief colloquy, at the end of which the senior of them, for the last time addressing Narvaez, said:

"Hermes Sforza, you are convicted by the evidence, and by your admission, of a crime whose punishment in every land is death. It is as vain to interrogate you upon the motives which induced your abominable resolve, as to question you further about your comrade. He will be taken, and of you, meanwhile, a prompt example shall be made. The Council takes into consideration every circumstance for and against you, and passes judgment without passion. The directness of your answers spares you the question; and the honor of your name, however you individually may have soiled it, induces us to remit the penalties which a common criminal would suffer. Had you been a Venetian, we should have spared the state the shame of knowing the baseness of one of her sons, and have caused your instant execution before us. But, as warning to foreign adventurers, our sentence is that you be returned to the cell whence you were brought, and that to-morrow, at the rising of the sun, you be taken, gagged as a malefactor, to the red pillars, and there strangled."

CHAPTER VI.

BETWEEN THE RED PILLARS.

Upon leaving the doge's presence, Hermes was conducted to the uppermost floor, where, on tapping at a small entrance, there appeared a clerical-looking individual, who was evidently prepared for their coming. The secretary paused but to address him in a hasty whisper; and by the time Hermes had glanced about, the door was closed and the doge's brother was gone.

The attic to which he had been guided was directly under a leaden roof, whereon the morning sun streamed with intense heat. He sat down upon a rough stool, of which there were several, and, burying his face in his hands, abandoned himself to a sombre meditation. Then, as the promise of escape returned, he sprang up and strode from one window to another.

At each his eye covered a wide panorama. From one could be seen the lagoon, and beyond it the Lido and the Adriatic, lying still and glassy in the breathless intensity of the summer heat, and with stationary sails upon the horizon; from another he beheld acres of tiled roofs, with curiously ornamented chimneys and weather-vanes, and here and there a covey of pigeons in the shade of some cornice; from the third was caught a peep at the mechanical bell-strikers of the famous clock-tower, and, far away in the northern distance, across the glare of sunlight, the glistening peaks of the Carnic Alps.

Then he looked at the man in whose custody he had been left, and whose austere face and simple garb had caused Hermes, when he first entered, to take him for some scrivener in the doge's private employ, to whom such confidential service might be entrusted. But a closer notice of the intellectual countenance, the delicate hands, the refined accent in speaking, and the dignified and courtly air, roused in him a momentary interest in the stranger.

The latter scrutinized Hermes with his great sad eyes, then a faint smile softened his thin and rigid lips as the thought came to him that so young and handsome a culprit had doubtless sinned through the customary offence of an ill-considered gallantry.

"Well, well," he said, with slow, deliberate utterance, and with a pleasant kindliness of manner, as though willing to touch this misadventure with the solace of resignation, "to one well favored as yourself all is not lost while love remains, and 'tis sure that neither the humblest nor the proudest woman in the world denies the sweetness of being its object. Yet in my own young days I noticed that men are no less vain than women, and that while women will die if they be not talked to about some quality they possess, that men delight most in hearing of the things they have not. To win a man of low order you have but to praise his intelligence. If he be a spendthrift, ask what's the news upon 'change. If he is old, and rheum-eyed, and gouty, quiz him upon his conquests with the fair."

"Alas!" replied Hermes to this apostrophe, "a sore heart has no humor to gossip; therefore suffer me to digest my trouble in silence, or, if you would give me food for reflection, be it of that substantial kind over which men differ less easily. I have not eaten more than a biscuit since yesterday's breakfast,—a vile one, as you will believe if you know the Osteria della Fame."

The stranger listened with a comical gesture of sympathy. "You will lodge little better here," he answered, "for there is no refectory in the palace, and the needs of my own appetite are infinitely small."

"It is not your appetite but mine own I feel for: no refectory in the palace! poor starvelings, has it come to that in Venice? Were we in the castle of Milan I could tell a different story; but on the piazza are cooks' shops,—the last thought of my freedom was of a collop of beef and a bird; surely, something can be brought me."

"And you think it would not attract the keen eyes of suspicion were I, who for two days have lived like the pigeons, to set myself ordering collops of beef?"

The last words arrested Hermes' attention. "You have lived here but two days?" he queried in surprise.

"Ay, two days that seem as months."

"I took this for your abode. Are you, too, in hiding?—have we both tried to assassinate the——"

"Assassinate!" interrupted the other with every mark of horror. "They told me you were guilty of some trivial fault. Holy St. Theodore, what purification can suffice to cleanse me from all these worldly stains?"

"Of what monstrous things have you been guilty?" ejaculated Hermes. "One would think you had committed the unpardonable sin."

The Venetian started at the words, as if he heard in them the condemnation of his own conscience.

"Woe is me!" he exclaimed, joining his hands and twisting his sinewy fingers together; "that chance utterance of a stranger speaks the words that ring in my ears night and day—the unpardonable sin!—the unpardonable sin——."

"And what is the unpardonable sin?" ventured Hermes, awestruck by the other's despair; "tell me, that I may profit by your warning and avoid it."

The Venetian glanced sharply about him, as one in habitual dread of eavesdroppers; then, turning upon Hermes his eyes, which an extraordinary excitement filled with a glow akin to the light of insanity, he asked in an abrupt whisper:

"For whom do you take me?"

"At first I thought you some trusted clerk, to whose confidence my safety was committed; but since you have been only two days in this dreadful garret, and acknowledge the guilt of a nameless crime, it occurs to me that you may be a fugitive like myself."

"*The guilt of a nameless crime and a fugitive!* Alas, yes. You have read my wretched life like an open scroll. Listen.

"In my youth I was an officer in the Venetian service, and commanded troops in the Levant. Beside the glory of conquest, it was my ambition to share the higher reward of those who piously recovered the relics of the Saints who had suffered martyrdom in the cities within our reach. To discover the missing ribs of St. Theodore was my constant preoccupation. One soft afternoon, as I walked along the street of a Saracen town we had captured, the thought filled my mind with unusual intensity. The palm branches rustled faintly in the breeze; ahead of me, down a vista of bazaars, strolled an Egyptian merchant; from behind a harem lattice peeped the laughing faces of two young girls ; and at the balcony of a spire whose gilded point glittered like a lance-head held aloft, leaned a friar ringing the Ave Maria from a Christian bell suspended upon the Moslem shaft. And through the vague sound of that faint tinkling, and with the solemn measure of waves breaking in ocean caves, came the voice of St. Theodore himself, speaking to me in accents of reproof for thinking more of the sanctified dead bones of others than of the living flesh of my own evil nature, and I stood rooted to the ground while he imposed upon me the vows of celibacy and of poverty, for the glory of God. And when the words were spoken, I beheld, as before, the merchant strolling idly down the street of shops, and the indistinct faces laughing behind the netting of the harem window, and heard again, though now with new and consecrated meaning, the soft, sweet summons to prayer.

"And after ten years spent in a monastery near the Alps, the Senate recalled me. You may well look amazed! My family, which in past generations gave a doge and rendered some service to the state, was about to become extinct. And therefore Venice commanded me to forswear my vow and renounce the life which St. Theodore had appointed, and marry. And, as a servant of my

native city, I obeyed, and I have lived three years
in the wedlock that to me was forbidden, and in
the house that was my home are two infant boys
to perpetuate my name. But ever the voice of St.
Theodore rang in my ears—'*The unpardonable sin,
the unspeakable sin*'—and three days ago I left all,
and having confided my secret to Barbarigo, even
as I have told it unto you, wait now till an opportunity is found to send me back to the Monastery—
well named—of Love Divine."

Hermes listened in silence to this grotesque and
heartless tale. It required no effort of the fifteenth-century mind to conceive this strange character, to admire its bigoted and fanatical mania,
and to construe as saintly heroism the cruel and
tragic selfishness of the end. The possessions of
this man's new life could have seemed to him no
nearer and no more significant than are fading
sails on the horizon to the voyager; not even the
prattle of his babes had drowned the mystical
admonition of St. Theodore; not all the tender
bonds of home and love had availed against the
fervent summons that floated ceaselessly from monastic cloisters, and that must have touched him
infinitely and irresistibly—even as the faint pealing of church bells, borne o'er the sea at sunset,
thrills forever the heart of Dante's mariner, outward bound.

An hour passed heavily away. A servant brought

them a frugal repast, and, this disposed of, Hermes threw off his silken doublet and walked the room, pausing now and again at the windows to catch the breaths of air that stirred. After mid-day the heat became excruciating, and he paced to and fro with flushed face, and the moisture standing upon his brow, and his eyes vacant, and his hands clenched together, as there rose incessantly before him the image of Narvaez, alone and defenceless, before that terrible tribunal. As the day drew to a close, and the flaming sunset faded to emerald on the horizon, his nervous striding up and down sank to a measured tread, while now and then he paused to observe the diminishing daylight, fancying how infinitely sad must be its vanishing from the dungeon bars through which Narvaez was doubtless watching it.

The Venetian sat unheeding, in motionless abstraction, all the day. At dusk he rose, and, producing flint, steel, and tinder, was about to light the end of a twisted taper, when a thought of the possible risk for Hermes of showing a light in that unfrequented part of the palace deterred him. A moment after the door opened, and, in the obscurity, the doge's brother entered.

His first words brought infinite relief. Narvaez had escaped the question, and was to be substituted for another prisoner whose trivial fault the doge could condone.

"But if Barbarigo can substitute and pardon whom he will, why not release Narvaez at once?"

"Because your offense is beyond pardon; the other prisoner, who is a youth of his own age, is held upon a petty accusation—some private vendetta which can be dismissed."

"How is it possible that he can put one prisoner in another's place?"

At this innocent question the secretary laughed sardonically. "Have you never heard of such things in Milan?" was his only reply.

"But you say Narvaez is condemned to death?"

"It is true."

"Then this other youth will suffer in his place."

"Cosa vuole! what would you? that is the way of the world."

"And Narvaez?"

"Will be released in the early morning, when the prison watch is changed, and conveyed in a gondola to the steps behind St. Mark's, within which, for greater safety, you and this gentleman will pass to-night; thence you will all be taken to Fusina, where suitable papers will pass you through the guards."

Some time after this comforting visit, the bells of the clock-tower rang out the hour, and the Venetian, rising, beckoned Hermes to follow.

"And whither?"

"Where Barbarigo's instructions summon—to pass the night in St. Mark's."

"And why not pass it here?"

"Because we could not leave in the morning without attracting notice, even if we got out at all."

"How, then, are we to leave St. Mark's?"

"After it is closed, at midnight, the keys are hung in the sacristy. Fear not but we shall find it a trusty hiding-place."

They reached the menials' stair, felt their way down its winding and unlighted length, and, after a descent that in the obscurity seemed interminable, emerged beneath the arches and looked out over the piazza upon the crowd that sat and strolled and talked along its brilliant extent. The distance to the vestibule of the church was only fifty paces, but neither dared risk the scrutiny of eyes that might be watching. They therefore turned into an alley, and, crossing a bridge, walked guardedly along a dim passage, lighted at the corners by candles flickering before saintly images, whereof not a few had already burned to the end, leaving saints and street alike in darkness.

As they again emerged upon the canaletto there arose the sound of exquisite music—the tinkling cadenças of mandolins, the thrumming of the guitar of Castile, and the voice of a lover serenading with the thrilling inspiration of Italian song. A slow, sweet prelude rose and fell with amorous pathos and passion, and Hermes ventured nearer till he beheld a gondola with flaring torches and indistinct forms reflected in the motionless water, and pointed windows and sculptured reliefs and frescoed colonnades above.

The music sank to a pleading intensity, and rippled away. To Hermes that quaint old song of the Sunbeam and the Rose was familiar: often had he heard it sung, in Milan, in the twilight of languorous evenings, by strolling minstrels in whose pipes and lutes and vibrant voices the populace delighted.

Reclining low on a mossy bed, through the summer's dreamy repose,
Blushing at noonday a deeper red, lay the lustre of earth—a Rose:
As fair as a hope of to-morrow, as sweet as a dream of to-day,
She knew not the autumn of sorrow, nor the freezing touch of decay.

A Sunbeam parting the leaves above stole softly through creeper and vine,
And whispering words of burning love cried, "Rose, darling Rose, thou art mine!"
But ending their fondest embraces, and quenching the thrill of delight,
Fell a veil that dispels and effaces, with the shadowy languors of night.

As Man reverts to the brilliant past, when the day we call
"Life" is done,
So, as the Sunbeam faded at last, the Rose turned to the setting
sun;
And the evening breeze idling near her caught a murmur it
echoes yet,
That was partly a sob of rapture, and partly a sigh of regret.

Ere the song ended Hermes and his companion had reached a side-door of St. Mark's. They walked, in almost complete darkness, down the pavement which the reverential tread of millions had already worn to unevenness, and concealed themselves in an obscure corner. Only two candles and the lurid spark of a lamp burned on the altar. They could distinguish faint silhouettes of the glimmering spans of the roof, and the sculptured chancel with iron rail twisted and beaten into fantastic shapes, and the line of ivory-white apostles, and beyond them the bronze statues of the illustrious dead. The altar stood out in spectral prominence, and upon the tracery of its carved and figured surface the moonlight, slanting through lofty windows of illuminated glass, laid soft, transparent coloring in feathery shafts of lemon, and sprays of clear sea-green, and stains of ruby, passing to pearly tints of sapphire, all which, when falling thus within a sacred precinct, the pious contadini call, "the flowers of the Virgin Madonna."

Exhausted beyond endurance, Hermes soon fell

into a slumber, from which he was awakened by the steady and ominous tolling of one of the great bells above. At the head of the church more lights had appeared, and several figures were moving. He started with a throb of despair at the thought of discovery, but beside him sat the Venetian, alert and attentive, and in the chancel was seen nothing more threatening than a venerable bishop, who advanced in full view, while about him clustered attendant priests and choristers. Having performed the usual genuflections before the altar, he faced the few people who had gathered, silent and awestruck, in the body of the church, while the choir began a shrill chant from one of the Psalms of David:

"Set thou a wicked man over him, and let Satan stand at his right hand.

"When he shall be judged, let him be condemned: and let his prayer become sin.

"Let his days be few, and let another take his office.

"Let his children be fatherless and his wife a widow.

"Let his children be continually vagabonds and beg; let them seek their bread also out of desolate places.

"Let the extortioner catch all that he hath, and let strangers spoil his labor.

"Let there be none to extend mercy unto him; neither let there be any to favor his fatherless children.

"Let his posterity be cut off, and in the generation following let their name be blotted out."

Hermes recognized the function of the major excommunication, and knew these words to be the preliminary summoning up of the sinister images wherewith, in olden days, the Church afflicted the souls of men. The chant ceased, and the bishop entered upon a lengthy recital of the pains and penalties which followed body and soul of one excluded from the fold, the priests answering at intervals in chorus. On earth the excommunicated was prohibited from entering a place of worship, and, this life ended, his spirit was consigned to Satan. He was denied the sacraments; he could not marry while living, nor be interred when dead; he was "a putrid member to be severed from the body of the faithful;" he was to be shunned as a leper; and whoever held converse with him, or relieved his necessity, or harbored him in peril, or took compassion upon his hunger, became a partner in his guilt and incurred the like anathema. As Hermes peeped from his hiding-place and heard these weird denunciations, it seemed to him, in his starved and forlorn condition, as if they were directed against himself, and were already in a fair way to fulfilment.

A lighted candle of yellow wax was now placed, with profuse reverences, in the hands of the officiating bishop, and smaller tapers were distributed among the attendant priests. A pause followed, during which the church bells were noisily rung in discord, as emblematic of the alarm and unrest which should thereafter possess the soul of him about to be named. Then the bishop proclaimed the unfortunate who had incurred these manifold distresses, and slowly and impressively pronounced the sentence:

"I excommunicate him; and as the light of this candle is now extinguished, so may the light of the Church be lost to him, and his soul be damned forever!"

And, thus speaking, he dashed his candle violently to the ground, and the priests, casting down those which they held, repeated after him:

"His soul be damned forever!"

The church was thereby left in its original obscurity. The company that had gathered dispersed with many crossings and bendings of devout knees. The bishop and his assistants withdrew, the bells no longer sounded, an acolyte busied himself with the covering of the altar, and the sacristan began the closing of the doors.

The night passed; the barking and howling of dogs on the piazza ceased, and a sombre day dawned as Hermes raised himself, bruised and stiff, from fitful snatches of sleep, to an awakening worse than the distorted visions of the night. The day passed in dim, cold streaks through lofty windows, and the first sound that reached him was the pattering of raindrops. The mechanical figures on the clock-tower hammered out the hour of five, and, in obedience to a gesture from his companion, he walked noiselessly to the main entrance, in the door of which was its great bronze key. They passed the vestibule, and looked across the piazza to the two historic pillars, between whose shafts had been, for centuries, the place of public execution. Already half a dozen men from the prison stood there in the rain, adjusting a rope.

Beneath that lowering sky Venice presented a dreary aspect: the deserted pavement glistened in the wet, and only the pigeons stirred beneath the arcades, or peeped from their shelter along the eaves.

Despite the nervous fatigue following upon hunger, sleeplessness, and anxiety, Hermes was alert and keenly watchful. He believed that his own deliverance was at hand, and that, at the appointed hour, Narvaez would be released. But, for a moment, a great excitement absorbed and detained him, for it was evident that an innocent life was to be sacrificed.

He did not long remain in suspense: a file of halberdiers emerged from the palace, and with them came a black-veiled executioner, and in their midst walked the youth who was to pay the forfeit of Narvaez's escape, and, on each side, a religious brother of the order whose office it was to accompany the condemned to execution. His arms were pinioned, his ankles chained, and across his mouth was a scarf covering the gag wherewith the Council stifled his utterance. The figure was slender, like the fencer's; the step, the hair, the very dress were his.

A violent tremor fell upon Hermes as the escort passed to where the men were waiting with silken cords. He understood it all now—but too late: the doge had deceived him—it was Narvaez who stood there—and in his helplessness his lips quivered, his eyes filled with tears, his brain reeled, he dropped upon his knees, and commenced an inarticulate recital of prayers. The veiled headsman's work was dexterously finished; to the last the monks muttered their supplications for the dying, while, in accordance with his sentence, the culprit was strangled between the pillars which bear the emblems of ancient Venice, and, after a brief spasm, his inanimate body rested against the post to which it had been bound. And, at the instant, the Venetian touched Hermes on the shoulder, and together they hastened to the bridge behind St. Mark's, and there lay a swift barge with four rowers, and hidden under the awning sat some one, and Hermes sprang in with an oath eloquent of great joy, and the Venetian followed, and the boatmen pushed off without a word and plunged into the obscurity of the canal.

And it was indeed Narvaez who sat beneath the cover, pale and weary, but unharmed. And Hermes, not knowing, at the instant, in what words to put his feelings, cast his arms about the fencer's neck, and kissed him, after the Italian fashion, upon each cheek.

CHAPTER VII.

A PROPHECY OF THE STARS.

The twilight hour of a quiet evening was well advanced as Hermes Sforza and Narvaez separated at the gate of Milan; the fencer to return to his school of arms, and Hermes to announce the result of their journey to the duke.

At that moment Ludovico was awaiting the soothsayer, Almodoro, for whom he had sent upon receiving a despatch announcing the capture, by the French, of the garrison of Acnone, and revealing the dejection and lethargy of his generals. It was his purpose to hasten to Alessandria to restore the confidence of the army; but, in accordance with the prevailing habit, before taking a step of unusual moment, he first sought an admonition from the stars.

He had locked himself, for an hour's meditation, in a study as small as that preserved in Florence at the Casa Buonarotti, wherein, sixty years later, Michael Angelo designed. It was large enough for its occupant to take three strides; its one window looked upon the plain of Lombardy. For furniture there was a single chair, some shelves piled with letters and records, and a writing-table whereon rested a marvellous cabinet of drawers and niches and compartments, divided by miniature columns of cornelian and onyx, and within whose secret spaces the duke kept important papers. Opposite the window was a crucifix, and beneath it a chronological tablet of the days and months. To this cosey retreat he habitually withdrew when an undisturbed morning of study and reflection lay before him. No one intruded upon his privacy; his memoranda and reports were there; and he derived a peculiar mental comfort from his narrow peep, between gables and chimneys, upon the outer world, where an occasional passer went hurrying by, and where, on gusty afternoons, he could watch the shrivelled leaves blown from the ground and carried upward and away, till they disappeared like birds that the eye can follow no more.

The iron-bound door of this diminutive retreat opened into a gallery of arms, wherein the duke occasionally crossed practice swords with some fencing-master, and which was hung with weapons and coats of mail, comprising his personal equipment. In the centre, mounted upon prancing wooden horses, were the gorgeous historic suits of his ducal ancestors, dating from the massive cuirass and casque of Muzio Attendolo, his condottiere grandfather. Along the walls were the helmets and breastplates and iron gauntlets, then gradually falling into disfavor, and the arquebuses and pistols that were taking their place. At each end was a complicated panoply of blades, from slender stilettos and broad hunting-knives, to Spanish rapiers and great gilded swords of state.

A sudden gathering of extreme dangers had disturbed in Sforza that calm which education and long self-mastery had fixed upon an ardent nature. To an irresponsible prince of mediaeval times, whose life and fortune were at stake, alliances and wars were of more earnest import than they sometimes seem to be to the talkative popular governments of the present. The usurper of Milan had, thus far, made his way with dexterous application of the subtle precepts of Italian statecraft. His breadth of view, his discrimination in dealing with men, the depth and astuteness of his political combinations, command the admiration of contemporary writers, and, among the Lombard people, his talents were for two centuries a subject of legendary tradition. But now he stood with no ally, his army was unnerved by a defeat, and in Milan prevailed whispers of treason that chilled the most constant.

In this extremity he summoned one who had been friend and counsellor, and who imposed upon his imagination by the possession of mysterious and marvellous gifts. In that superstitious and spirit-haunted age, astrology appeared before the terrors of humanity as an interpreter of incomprehensible phenomena. The most learned were beguiled by arts which bewildered the senses, and fascinated with the lure of a glimpse into futurity.

The duke had idled away the afternoon in uneasy reveries, now seated in his little study, now passing to the library beyond, and watching from an open window for the first appearance of the stars. At length, unable to endure the phantasms with which a nervous excitement filled his solitude, he despatched a page to hasten Almodoro's coming.

The alchemist was found in the laboratory in which he pursued the fantastic researches to which the votaries of occult science were self-dedicated, and whose toil they prized above all earthly pleasure, each one believing that he held a mystic thread issuing from the starlight of antiquity and leading to the dominion of the future. This laboratory was a large, square room, with a vast oven, and shelves of manuscript books, originally copied from the Ptolemaic rolls in the Alexandrian library, and alcoves crammed with odd instruments, and glass retorts, and drugs, and essences, and meteoric stones, and uncouth petrifactions, such as would have filled the eyes of a peaceable citizen of that period with wonder. His chief treasure was a divining chart which had come down from the Greek sorcerers—sole surviving fragment of the books of "them which used curious arts," whereof Paul and Silas made so famous a bonfire.

The alchemists were men of superior attainments, who possessed scientific knowledge in advance of their age. They were apt mechanics in the construction of philosophic instruments; they must be geologists, botanists, mineralogists, chemists, mathematicians, and astronomers. All this collective knowledge, with the addition of Oriental magic and astrologic divination, they applied to their search for an elixir of perpetual youth, and for a method of converting the baser metals into gold.

Through the complex theories woven by generations of students, and across centuries of experiment, Almodoro had patiently traced and retraced a devious path. He had devoted years to the study of magnetism, and to analyzing the principles of suspended animation, which, he supposed, could be infinitely developed. In the presence of death he had repeatedly attempted a transfer of vitality from one person to another, but so exquisite was the nicety required for this performance that on more than one occasion, between fright and collapse, both subjects had slipped through his incantations into eternity.

Ludovico advanced to meet Almodoro as he

entered the library, and looked into his face with earnest inquiry.

"I have suffered a day of torment," he began, taking the astrologer abruptly by the arm, and leading him to seats beside an open window.

"What is amiss?" queried the seer, with the frank utterance of a familiar friend. "You do not doubt that I am ready as ever, yet your importunities this afternoon indicate almost a mistrust. Surely you know that only at certain conjunctions can a forecast be made."

"At the worst I have brought you here but an hour too soon, and I could endure my unrest no longer."

"For shame! he that conquers himself is greater than the Duke of Milan. Only to think that the novitiate through which I led you towards an intellectual sovereignty more valuable than earthly powers should prove thus futile."

The duke's countenance fell at this rebuke from a nature stronger than his own.

"I have been ill," he answered, "and your ingenious formulas avail little to one who lacks your flinty being. For me, every circumstance that I brooded over took on a misproportion, and made me long to know what new signs must be written since we deciphered the portents three years ago."

"Take courage," answered Almodoro, laying his

hand caressingly upon Ludovico's; "it is a trite saying that, in this queer world, the extremity of grief is often the beginning of joy."

Sforza clasped both hands over his eyes as though to shut out some pursuing presence; then, dashing them down, he exclaimed:

"It is yet time to remedy all. If your words favor I shall leave in the morning for Alessandria. Let us to the terrace—is it too soon? Then, while we wait, answer me a question I had in my thoughts all day. You have told me of your wanderings and of wondrous places and strange men. Found you ever a scholar who could trouble your faith in your arts?"

"What childish words are these? The truths I have unfolded to you were true to the Priests of Philae, to the Druids of Britain, to the Magi of Atlantis, as they are to-day to the few patient and zealous students that remain."

"I marvel not the alchemists are few," murmured Ludovico, "after my own apprenticeship."

"For that matter," replied Almodoro, "neither do I. You were warned at the outset that not one ordinary man in a million could survive even that preliminary discipline which purifies our infirm bodies and leads the perfected spirit to that plane where it gradually becomes superior to the mutations of nature. The Buddhist who has attained this faculty has the power of walking upon water or of floating through the air; yet how trivial are these vagaries beside the refined influence through which the process of natural decline is averted. The alchemist has quenched every human passion and attachment. Only one flame remains, and this is a reflex of the halo which encircles our mystic cabala. Only he who has lived such a life can judge of its spiritual compensations, its intimate communings with secret principles, its fine perceptions of the mystery of its own being. Before such a one stretch infinite cycles of experience and discovery. He will follow the growth of nations and outlive them; he will watch the progress of merely human learning and its decline; he will see the rise of new religions and their decadence. And, borne irresistibly onward by the vast and subtle forces he has conquered, he will pass the seas to the dominion of yet untrodden continents, and pluck from the Golden Indies of Columbus the forbidden attributes which the ancients sought in vain."

The duke started from his half-recumbent ease, apparently intending to break in upon this abstruse discourse with an inquiry, but the soothsayer went on without heeding:

"Nor can you discover anything contrary to reason," he continued, "in the principles I taught you. It is often said, 'Such a one is old, but he retains his faculties and the vigor of his body.'

There is no greater marvel than that he has not abused them by contradicting those simple rules of longevity, whose minute observance is the alchemist's elementary lesson. Fancy this habit multiplied an hundredfold in the hourly enforcement of a system both mental and physical, and one of two things results: either the novice dies insane, or, if the stars favored his birth in an extraordinary degree, the functions of brain and body may go on for centuries. There is a time in life when the production and exhaustion of the body are equal, when, consequently, there is no loss, no diminution. The Chaldeans began with the inquiry why this balance could not be indefinitely continued; the alchemist has answered by successfully preserving this subtle poise of his forces. And similarly it has required ages to discover that beyond all human knowledge, which is but an attempt to hide the shame of ignorance, the mind has powers which, when developed, reveal the secrets of the universe. So truly as the transmutation of metals is true, so certainly is perfected man capable of renewing youth. If humanity lives upon the lees of nature, it was none the less our primeval destiny to be of an unchanging vitality, drawing vigor from the elements about us, and no more susceptible to decay than the sunlight or the ocean. At first, when this tremendous possession is ours, we seem to hold all the powers of the infinite; we learn to govern ourselves in proportion as we perceive that our actions make and unmake our happiness. We find that their effect follows us in regret or in contentment, even through immortality; that it passes with us, day by day, the lines which separate the present from the infinite hereafter, and from the past; out of the twilight of bygone years come to us the spectres of bad and ignoble actions. From them we learn to live as men who have risen above the temptation of their own infirmity."

Ludovico interrupted this discourse with a bitter laugh.

"I can so far agree with you," he said, "that these last days have shown that, even in my failure, there remains a spark that can yet be warmed to some purpose. You remember that Barbarigo, of Venice, and I were novices together; we took the degree of fellowship, and assumed the obligation that binds your sect for life,—or. if you prefer, forever. We both proved unequal to the ordeal, I thinking I should presently become demented, he fearing he was to be delivered over to the devil. We both returned to the commonplace of Earth, but the impressions of that extraordinary schooling remained, and the oath which bound us never to do one another a mischief continued. No one could escape the solemnity with which that vow was assumed, and the fearful penalties we each invoked if it were broken. Barbarigo remembers, and is faithful. In my extremity I adjured him, by the pledge of our youth, to relieve me; and so much vigor remains in the memory of that ghostly experience that, at the risk of life, he engages to halt the Venetian troops on the frontier. Hermes has just returned and has told me the story.—But come, we lose time; let us to the terrace. If your arts have value, you shall this night give me straightforward answers."

The elevation upon which they emerged was a balustraded roof, the approaches to which Ludovico bolted before following his companion.

"How long it seems," he ejaculated, as they stood together, "since we read the heavens; 'twas a few weeks before her death, well-nigh three years ago."

"You blamed me then—you blame me now—for that sad misfortune," answered the alchemist; "you would have taken my head had I not escaped."

"I but held you responsible for the failure of one of your devices."

"But I was not responsible for a thing I did against my judgment, under the extreme pressure of your wife's entreaty, enforced by your own command. Remember all that happened, and do me justice. The child had been born a month; from the first its life had been prolonged with infinite pains from day to day, almost from hour to hour. Slowly that little spark had paled, till, one night when I was summoned, I saw that it could not survive till dawn. Your wife besought me at any cost—those were her words—to save it. You have never known what I did; you would listen to no explanation at the time; in a moment of weakness I imparted to her a secret of our science—the prolongation of one life by the sacrifice of another; to be surrendered, not merely voluntarily, but with an intensity that translates its very essence. She passed, at the hearing, from despair to an heroic self-possession which I conjured her to preserve. I warned her, above all, not to fear for herself. I promised that, through the watches of the night, I would not leave her; that, at the moment when the child had received the requisite vitality, I would arrest its flow. I was a fool to imagine that unpurified humanity can exercise the loftiest acts of calm and courage. An hour went by; slowly the babe revived, as, by an intense volition, the mother's life passed to it. Then the color faded from her own face; she became unconscious—of a sudden I beheld the pallor of death. In vain I essayed to suspend the flow of animation,—something baffled my efforts,—finally she opened her eyes and murmured, as one who acknowledges a fault: 'I did not fear, but I doubted.' Alas! that doubt ruined all; there she lay dead, with the infant asleep in her arms. My failure was followed by an instantaneous relapse in the child—look up yonder, high in the second division, you can see them both together—one large and bright, with a generous beam, the other small and twinkling—they are there, mother and child."

For these astrological calculations of old, the firmament was conceived as an inverted dome, covered with figures, signs, and letters, through whose shifting relations the master could decipher past, present, and future. Almodoro produced a paper on which were traced certain lines which Ludovico recognized to be the magnetic latitudes of the three regions — Empyrium, Æthereum, and Elementary.

The wise man fixed his attention upon the stars, occasionally bending down to trace upon the paper a line, or to make a point, whose significance was vaguely guessed by his companion; gradually it grew to be a chart of Sforza's life; in its centre a hieroglyph bearing the date of his birth; and every curve and dot made by the soothsayer rendered sufficiently distinct by the lamplight, which streamed upon the table from the window behind.

"How marvellous a scroll is spread above us," softly observed Almodoro, his mind filled with the zest of his pursuit; "do you remember my explaining the indications of the freaks of destiny?

Behold how salient they are to-night; yonder there is a beautiful girl in the promise of life—see, she is about to be clutched by a disease that hovers near; to the right a stalwart cavalier, with seemingly brilliant future, will be cut down in some paltry skirmish to-morrow; and, stranger than these, mark you there, low on the horizon, that lengthening line,—those are lives whose drift is aimless and which rust on in sloth. Seems it not strange that one should find, written among the stars, even the ignoble caprices of Fate?"

"Be these trifles as you please, let us to our purpose."

"There is but one serious change: all is much as we found it three years ago, except for a great and newly declared peril; follow me on this chart and read for yourself. The line of your life begins on the ascendant; in early manhood comes a crisis; the line is violently agitated; all this marks the first accession; here comes again an extreme peril."

"Well, and after that?"

"The line begins a long, undeviating course."

"All this means that I stand in imminent danger; that, if I escape, I have a long future before me?"

"Yes, a dozen years at least."

"Will they be prosperous years?"

"They bear an aspect of great calm, as though little troubled by the world."

"Give me no Delphic utterance; shall I go to Alessandria to-morrow?"

"It is unsafe to approach a battlefield."

"But is the danger one that belongs to a battlefield?"

"It is obviously connected with the present war."

"But I may be assassinated during the present war."

"That would still come under the portent of arms and the shock of battle, all which is plain to see."

"How ends the battle plain to see is it a victory or a defeat?"

"It begins auspiciously; at its conclusion I behold you standing with several French officers in view perhaps the captive chiefs of the enemy."

"Io triumphe!" cried the duke, raising his hands in exultation. "Methinks I see the renegade Trivulzio before me. But hark ye, Almodoro, your forecast is unusually hedged about with doubts. Cannot the stars be made to tell an unequivocal tale?"

"Ludovico, I tell you what I read and the inferences to be drawn; to do more we must resort to that for which I know your aversion,—we must summon a familiar."

"What! conjure up a lesser devil, and bid him speak the truth?"

"I did not say a devil; I mean a benignant presence."

"I have not known a benignant presence since Beatrice died. Had you power to bring her spirit into communion with mine, I might receive some admonition."

"Then let us return within, for our task here is accomplished, and you are weary."

"I once sought in vain," said Sforza, after they had seated themselves in the library, "to see a well-known spirit. I rested a night, some years ago, at the castle of Rimini, and, after supper, we talked of Francesca; and one present, who was a scholar, repeated the lines wherein Dante describes her spectre floating through realms of twilight, till, as the evening wore on, I went out to breathe the crisp air. From the gate leads a promenade along which Francesca and Paolo may have passed in the old romantic days; and within a half circle of venerable trees is a stone bench, covered with lichens, upon which they may have read together the idyl of Launcelot and Guinevere. I found myself possessed by the mystic influence which tradition weaves about the place; you may say that it was but the transition to the midwinter gloom of the hedgerows from the great wood-fire that blazed in our dining-hall; but when something sighed in the branches, and an owl flew hooting away, I fully believed I should behold Francesca and her lover revisiting the scene which memory makes dear to them forever."

As the duke spoke he became conscious of a slight oppression; he looked towards Almodoro and beheld the alchemist's gaze fixed intently upon him. Then Ludovico's eyes closed, and in fancy he beheld the broad garden by the Adriatic, where, concealed in an arbor, he had waited and watched one day, eight years ago, for the first glimpse of the maiden Beatrice, his bride that was to be, who, all unconscious of his presence, should presently stroll down the walk.

An enchanted vision recalled the slumbrous stretch of the amaranth-tinted sea, and the olives that bent above him, and the flowering vines that crept to their branches.

And, as on that day when first he beheld her, she appeared,—a tall, graceful figure, with pensive face and lustrous eyes,—unchanged and beautiful as ever. He heard the rustle of her lilac satin gown, and noticed the head-dress of her girlhood, the pointed crimson beretta, with gauze floating behind, the tight, golden sleeves of her dress, the chatelaine suspended at her girdle, and the bunch of honeysuckle unfaded in her hand after all these years.

It was an apparition that, even in his dream,

thrilled Ludovico as deeply as on that well-remembered day. But now he watched for some endearing sign, or some prophetic utterance, for the eyes met his with wistful and intense desire. But the figure vanished with no other token than that eloquent gaze, and Ludovico awoke and beheld Almodoro. The duke was still blinded by the dazzling splendor of that southern sea, and the smell of spectral orange blossoms lingered in his nostrils as he exclaimed:

"O Almodoro, I have seen Beatrice! and there was a gentle melancholy upon her face, and she looked upon me fixedly, as though her heart were bursting to speak; but she passed in silence, without sign or token,—and often have I heard you say that this portends some great, some terrible misfortune!"

CHAPTER VIII.

A REVELATION.

The Italian of four centuries ago lived under influences widely different from those which mould his voluble descendant. In the midst of a graceful and cultivated civilization blazed feuds and strifes whose alarms and sufferings were the commonplace features of existence. Often confronted by stirring and tragic events, and free from the accessories and distractions of modern ease, people were less given to reading and talking than to thought and action. In the Middle Ages men and women faced danger frequently, and learned not merely to confront it with self-command, but to pluck some ingenious resource even from desperation itself. Hence grew those habits of reticence, of self-restraint, of dissimulation, which speak from the intent, watchful, furtive portraits of the Quattro Cento.

Amid the whirl of such swift achievement and sudden reverse as fill the pages of mediæval history, had Bernardino Corte passed his life. The contemplation of one idea in many aspects had made him reserved and abstracted. He had mused upon the decline of the Visconti, and their succession by the upstart Sforza in Milan; he had watched the creation of little states along the Adriatic; he had seen how individuals swayed the Guelph and Ghibelline masses at Florence; he had laughed to observe at Rome the humblest condottiere captains acquiring vast possessions, and converting their sobriquets to patrician-sounding names. And, consumed by that vanity which sometimes stirs mediocrity to reckless deeds, he sought the chance to carve a soldier's fortune. In the impending collapse of the House of Sforza he recognized his opportunity, and promised himself to rise from the vortex upon his master's shoulders. Inseparably linked with his political aims was the wild aspiration to win the imprisoned duchess, and, by a marriage with this daughter of royalty, to attain a pinnacle equal to the loftiest dream.

The transition had not been difficult from the inspection of a captive to an impulsive sympathy, and thence to an occasional visit, when the governor would beguile an hour in telling of his wondrous travels in the Levant, of the doings in Milan, of the painters and writers whose names were becoming famous, of his own dabblings at authorship; how a companionship formed itself between him and his characters; how he thought for them, spoke for them, shaped their actions, and, in fancy, shared their peril and measured the temptation of their love. Or, again, he talked of music, of the latest barcarole of the Venetian gondoliers, and he would take the lute which rested against the wall, and, after some tuning of the unused strings, touch them in vibrating swell of full accords, and sing, till, for an instant, Isabelle forgot her sorrows, and strayed, where the song led, down the long walk of some romantic glade, or out upon the Adriatic, amid the sparkle of the sunshine and the sea.

Accustomed as the duchess had been to the fascination exercised by the witchery of her presence, she was not slow to divine the motive of these advances. In the first discouragement of evil days she repelled them with aversion, but, as months went by, the thought repeated itself that, under Ludovico, the governor was supreme in the castle; that the future might bring political vicissitudes; that, with better fortune and a pliant jailer, escape might be achieved and the sceptre recovered.

After several years the changes for which jailer and captive had watched with the same envious longing, though from different points of view, had come. And now that the imminent overthrow of Ludovico marked the hour for the unfolding of his designs, Bernardino sought the duchess one evening, in the determination to make their interview decisive. He was conscious that never before had so delicate a task confronted him, but the ardor of his infatuation was stimulated by the very distance that held them apart. Often in bygone days he had paced the starlit streets, meditating upon the obduracy which met every advance; but to-night he nerved himself with the boast, familiar to such meditations, that he never yet had failed in any purpose to which the effort of his undivided powers had been applied.

The duchess received the governor with a kindly greeting at variance with her habitual indifference. She rose with the satisfaction of one who meets an expected friend, and Bernardino beheld, with wonder, that she had put off her sombre robes of mourning. He paused, cap in hand, an involuntary instant, seeking, in that moment's pause, to read the meaning of that smiling calm; the words framed in salutation faltered, and he remained gazing steadfastly upon the woman he loved, in her resplendent attire, and wearing above the heavy braids of her hair the coveted ducal fillet of gold.

"Your startled look is a rebuke upon me for these changed garments," she said, with sweet, musical utterance; "I know not why I have put on again this sad, old, faded gown; it must have been caprice, or perhaps the pulse of a hope for the future, the first hope,—oh, be it not my last! But draw near, wish me good-evening, and be seated."

The governor advanced, raised to his lips the hand she extended, and said with hesitation, "I come to speak upon matters we have somewhat talked of,—the times are so ominous, and the news so bad——"

"The news so bad! what is the news?"

"I cannot guess how much knowledge of the war has reached you, but——"

"I know all; what then?"

"The latest despatch from the front is couched in such terms," answered the governor very slowly, and observing her intently, as though to measure the effect his next words would produce, "that one might almost assume it equal to a declaration that everything is lost."

The duchess listened with eyes brimming, and with lips trembling with emotion, as one o'ercome with joy.

"Then God has heard the supplications of my despair," she murmured, "and I am saved!"

The governor bent compassionately over her, and ventured to lay his hand upon hers as he whispered:

"Our time is brief, too brief for tears or useless words; a great crisis has burst upon us, and it may present such an opportunity as comes but once in a lifetime; but for the moment we must think of your safety, and your boy's."

Isabelle looked up in feigned astonishment.

"What possible danger threatens here?" she asked.

"It requires courage nothing less than sublime," answered the governor, with eyes fixed intently upon the inquiring face uplifted to him, and speaking with a tinge of sarcasm, "to watch the approach of extreme peril with so much nonchalance. Or is it, perhaps, a child's heedlessness, which fears not because it does not understand?"

"Are you serious in these alarms?" exclaimed the duchess. "If so, speak plainly, I beseech you; and, as becomes a brave woman, I will listen to the worst."

"It is fortunate," replied Bernardino, "that in me you have a friend equal to any emergency. "Hark, what is this?—some one comes!"

The door of the adjoining room flew wide open as he spoke; and the boy Francesco, unconscious of the governor's presence, danced in, followed by a dog, about whose ears he had bound a handkerchief.

"See!" exclaimed the child gleefully, "he has on his nightcap, it is bedtime for us both."

"How well you love your four-legged playmate," said Bernardino, catching the child for an instant.

"He never scolds me," replied Francesco, explaining his affection as he watched the animal's efforts to clear itself.

"And will you always be happy together in this castle,—you and your dog?"

"While I am a boy, yes," replied Francesco dubiously.

"Then a time may come when you will be glad to leave us?"

"To be sure, when I am a man; for then I shall be Duke of Milan."

"Who says you will be Duke of Milan?"

"Mamma and my nurse."

"But your good uncle—is not he Duke of Milan?"

"I hate him," savagely answered the child, disengaging himself. "I hate you too," he added with rising color; "some day I will cut off both your heads!"

"Venomous little brute!" thought Bernardino. Then, turning to the duchess, with a smile, he said, "Your son has your own magnificent spirit, but, long before he puts these heroic resolves into action, he will have learned to distinguish those who wish him well." The door slammed violently as he spoke,—the boy and his favorite had taken unceremonious leave. The duchess heeded not his words, but returned to the point at which their talk had been interrupted. "Tell me something," she said, "of the danger whereof you began to speak."

"If I understand that question aright, it means that you ask my confidence."

The duchess bowed her head without speaking.

"In exchange for your own," pursued Bernardino.

"In exchange for mine," assented Isabelle simply.

"You say you know all; then you have been told of the massacre at Aenone."

"Every one but yourself has been talking of it these last five days."

"You have heard that a panic seized upon the Italians at Alessandria, that the troops believed themselves sold and became mutinous. And lastly comes a despatch that Sanseverino, unable to maintain his authority, and fearing his own soldiers more than those of King Louis, fled for his life, abandoning the army, whereupon followed a great confusion between those who would fight, others eager to yield, and all hurrying this way and that."

Isabelle had listened to the last sentence with breathless interest; she bent forward as Bernardino finished, and asked softly:

"And what says Ludovico to all this?"

"He is silent and moody,—consumed, as it were, by his own thoughts."

"But you share his thoughts," insisted the duchess, with earnestness and with coquettish insinuation; "what are they?"

"I know only what all know,—that to-morrow the great personages of Milan are to assemble in the Hall of the Signoria, where Ludovico will explain his administration and appeal to the citizens to stand by him."

Isabelle's face clouded with disappointment. "I thought you more generous," she said reproachfully, "towards a friend whom you declare you esteem, and in whom you know you can confide."

The governor shrugged his shoulders in vexed impatience at this reproach. But, on the instant, he checked his irritation and answered with unruffled composure.

"You do me injustice," he began; "you blame me for not knowing what cannot be divined; you take as nothing the indulgences by which you profit, each one of which is a breach of duty in me, and some whereof, were they detected, would imperil my life; you tolerate my presence as one endures an unavoidable intrusion; you do not even give me credit for magnanimity, in that I do not thrust upon you the words and the tokens of a passion that is breaking my heart."

The duchess laughed sardonically in his face. "A fine suitor!" she cried bitterly, "who leaves his darling in a dungeon to suffer insult and privation. Listen," she added, dropping her voice to a tone of infinite tenderness, and fixing upon him the appealing look of her Italian eyes; "if I were a man in your station, and loved a friendless and afflicted woman, I would hazard all to rescue her from the cruelty of her enemies; and, though I died for it,

I should feel reward in the knowledge that she could never after think of me without an emotion that would be somewhat akin to mine for her."

"That were cold comfort to a man in his grave."

"You cut a sorry figure with your fears for yourself and your empty words for me."

"Were this visit known to the duke, I should have good reason to fear, and if these empty words of ours could reach his ears, neither of us would live to see to-morrow's sun."

"Yet you can stand motionless in your own peril, and leave me helpless in mine. What shall I think of a man whom neither fear nor love can move?"

Stung to the quick by this retort, the governor entered at once upon the ruse with which he had prepared himself. The duchess, after her last reply, had moved from him to the end of the room. The windows were open, the night was still, the warm air bore in a vague sweetness of summer perfumes; they were alone, none could hear or interrupt, and Bernardino, with brain on fire, nerved himself for the moment which should shape his life.

He began abruptly, in a tone of nervous excitement. "Isabelle!" he exclaimed, addressing her for the first time by name, "this impossible situation must cease. I have come to-night to end it. I must speak, however briefly, of what you would not hear; if what I say displeases you, if you heed not my warning, I shall receive my final sentence without demur, and leave you to your fate."

The duchess faced him with calm deliberation, and, as he framed his next words, he thought her more beautiful than ever before, but colder than Diana as she stood there listening, attentive, unruffled.

"You have been to me an ideal," he began, "at the same time that your misfortune and your grief appealed to me as they must have touched the compassion of any man who had known your sorrow, or seen you helpless and forsaken. Such a passion as neither strength can master, nor absence change, nor disdain extinguish, grew within me. I bore my burden two years in silence. One afternoon that I came in from the joyous sunshine and the exuberant happiness of the flowering fields, your sadness, your tears, your apprehensions moved me beyond the repression I had imposed upon myself. I spoke, less as a lover than as a friend — and you banished me. My love was hopeless: you clung to the thought of one whose affection and whose memory were consecrated by the tribulations you had shared together, and by the solemn parting of his last hour. And yet the unworthy thought comforted me that, with your husband dead, and yourself in the grasp of a relentless enemy, without a soul to appeal to but your confessor and myself, you would be reduced to the extremity of despair, and that I should be recalled. Months passed—an explanation followed, and from that time you have tolerated my presence; nay, in my musings upon the theme never out of my thoughts, I have discovered signs that you are not wholly averse to me; that but for the empty memory you live for, and without the difference in our station, your heart and your soul would speak in answer to mine. And now, in the gathering of strange and terrible events, it is time to determine whether you value my love, or if you think to trifle with it in a way dangerous to us both."

"Dangerous!" ejaculated the duchess incredulously; "that is a forbidding argument with which to ingratiate yourself."

"Dangerous!" hissed the governor, made furious by her quiet disdain,—"fatal you will find it if you spurn me again."

"What mean these dark croakings?"

"That Ludovico never yet gave warning where or when he strikes. Ah! you begin to understand—you can at length be made to see that your own destiny hangs by his."

"Think you Sforza would dare harm me or Franceschino, when the French are about to take him by the throat?"

"Alas! what avails revenge to the dead?"

"The dead! heart of a fiend that you have, to torment me thus!"

"That which has been done before can be done again." answered Bernardino, launching his long-meditated shaft. "What availed the French to your husband, living or dead? did they even notice his death, or the manner of it?"

"What mean's? — why look you thus? One would think you meant——"

"Yes, I do mean it."

"That Galeazzo died poisoned! and it was you that suffered so vile an infamy to be accomplished, and you dare to come to me and talk of it in the same breath you declare your love!"

A silence fell upon them. The duchess stood with face averted, with lips convulsed, with moistened eyes, with fingers clenched in her handkerchief. The governor observed her attentively, considering the effect of the stroke upon which all depended.

"If the memory of an infinite wrong cannot stir you to more than tears," he said, stepping close to her, "surely the sense of a mortal danger to your child will arouse you. It is strange if you knew not what I have told you—that Galeazzo died at his uncle's command. That you blame me for his death is saying that you hold the absent responsible for what is done without their knowledge. But after all was over, I heard the circumstances of Galeazzo's end; I was told of the suddenness of the attack, of the cramps that baffled the leech you had summoned, of the sweat that bedewed his face as it flushed and paled alternately. That his death removed the last obstruction in Ludovico's path to the throne awakened the suspicion of many; crushed, persecuted, imprisoned as you were, you heard not the murmur of execration that rose from the populace. The usurper had held the sceptre as regent; now he sought the coronet for himself. One evening, in conference with the duke, I hinted at the taking off of Galeazzo as a secret I had readily divined, and he started, then looked grave, and answered, 'Necessity constrained me.' Since that night I have led him to speak of the details of his crime, how Landriano urged its commission, and how a juggling conjurer named Almodoro prepared the fatal drug. You know not the name of Almodoro, the duke's incessant companion? then to-morrow ask your confessor what he thinks of him, and, when you hear his answer, bear this in mind: that, his task accomplished, the magician vanished and has not been seen in the flesh from that time until a week ago; and why, think you, should he have returned from his remote hiding-place among the oriental masters of the black art, had not Ludovico summoned him for a second service,—he who did the first so well. Be warned in time. If Ludovico dared not put an end to three together, now, after a lapse of years, he will make bold to send the two that remain after the first.

The dreadful end of Galeazzo gathers about you and your child, and I, alone, can save you both."

With that intensity of volition possible to strong natures, the duchess stifled the emotion of so violent a shock and turned to listen.

Bernardino continued with increasing agitation. "Consent to be mine," he said, "to share the future with me, and you shall have a revenge so complete, that, from the ruin of Ludovico Sforza, we shall raise ourselves together to power and to the honors that should be yours, and when that much is reached my crime will be forgotten, and the Church will bestow its benediction upon us as man and wife."

"Your crime?" whispered the duchess, intent upon his words.

"Listen," pursued the governor, grown very pale, and speaking fast and low, as though to hasten through the mention of the infamy he had imagined.

"To me will be entrusted this castle, whose ramparts and whose treasures are now the last support that remain to Ludovico. If he hide within its shelter, he shall perish by my hand; if he fly, leaving me here to defend it, I will proclaim you duchess, and no foothold will remain to him in Italy."

"If you save me and set me free," answered Isabelle, "you shall have great reward; if you can persuade the French to restore Francesco, you shall name your own honors; but our fates are not the same, nor can they be happily joined."

"It shall be that or nothing. I know what is in your thoughts; you are saying to yourself, the daughter of a king weds not with the governor of a fortress. Do you then take no heed of the strange ups and downs that fill our time? Have you forgotten how the talents of the first Sforza lifted him to the place of the effete Visconti? So shall I, with a single leap, rise above the remnants of your house and make your dukedom mine. You know me not yet, nor do you measure the intensity of my nature. All my life I have followed few and simple aims, but I have always known my own purpose clearly, and that is a source of infinite strength. And I have loved but once—you, only you—and such love has an earnestness and an endurance and a purity that no woman can wholly withstand. Now, answer, will you and your child take the torment of Galeazzo's last hour from your enemy, or will you share my fortune and my crime with me?"

Isabelle's eyes fell at this question, and the answer demanded came not. Bernardino marked her irresolution, and, thinking her resistance exhausted, or her judgment overtempted, exclaimed passionately: "Speak!—choose between death and Milan!" And at the words the duchess bowed her head in assent and answered faintly, with the constraint of one who is forced to a decision:

"Since life is at stake, and since nothing less than the sacrifice of myself can save my child—be it as you require. But," she added, looking suddenly up with face changed from white to crimson, "you shall perform your task to the end before I see you again. When Ludovico is dead, or a fugitive, and this castle yours, come hither; and then, whatever the French king reserves for me shall be equally yours and mine."

He sprang toward her at the word with outstretched arms, as if to snatch an embrace from the lips that promised surrender; but with an imperious gesture she stopped him.

"Hark!" she said softly, pointing to the open window, "hear you not from afar the watchman's cry? he calls the hours and adds, '*All's well!*' O Bernardino, may that prove an omen of our future, and when all this is done, may we look into one another's eyes and say all's well."

The governor assented with a smile; then, with one swift, eloquent look upon her, left the room, and, as the door closed after him, he drew a long, deep sigh of nervous excitement, and muttered:

"It is done. I have but to strike, and all that the world can give is mine."

CHAPTER IX.

THE HALL OF THE SIGNORIA.

On the following morning the castle was astir with unwonted activity. It was Sunday, and the solemn gathering of the Signoria, or assemblage of prelates, nobles, and citizens, had been appointed to it, that the conclave and its resolves might borrow from the day something of its spiritual purpose. To this appeal had Ludovico resorted as a diversion wherewith to cajole from the Milanese a voluntary conscription and a half-involuntary loan; and to this end he was to review before them the favorable traits of his rule, and foreshadow the calamities which must attend the invader. He had designed to heighten the effect of this discourse by a dramatic release of the duchess, but, to Hermes' astonishment, Isabelle refused to leave her prison unless expelled by force.

Ludovico had prepared himself for this meeting with perfect confidence in its good effect. At a time when representative government was well nigh unknown, such a convocation was the most flattering of all the arts of political persuasion with which Machiavelli's typical prince could beguile his subjects; unfortunately it was also a confession of extreme weakness, for it was resorted to only in the direst straits.

The populace gathered in animated groups about the space between the castle and the city. The shopman, with party-colored jacket; the contadina, with white and yellow dress and silver shaft through her braids; the soldier, with leather doublet and iron casque; the black-robed scrivener's clerk, and his sweetheart, the milliner's maid; the swarthy artisans in their Sunday frocks, all jeered and chatted and craned over one another's shoulders, as, through their midst, walked the nobles followed by servants wearing their master's blazon, or, at intervals, a prelate attended by a couple of sacristans carrying over his head a purple umbrella; close upon the heels of these came the usurers, reluctantly obeying the summons, and glad to follow in the peaceful wake of the monsignori. While few escaped the gibes of the rabble, several who were known to oppose the duke were applauded.

The jesting and hooting subsided at the approach of a dust-covered retinue attending a mounted officer clad from the waist up in the knightly armor which was soon to become obsolete, and with helmet hanging at the saddle-bow. A muttered execration preceded him, for he was Sanseverino, the luckless commander of Ludovico's army, who had fled after a first misfortune, leaving his regiments to disperse. He sat his horse with fine bearing, for in the lists he possessed a prowess which, with an address in handling troops on the parade ground, had won for him the repute of an accomplished general. Irritated at the taunts of the populace, he spurred his horse to a trot, and, followed by the escort which had accompanied him from Alessandria, disappeared within the castle. While stretching himself after his fatigues in the saddle, and listening to an explanation of the unwonted throng on the piazza, he despatched his seneschal to ask audience of the duke. His messenger was promptly conducted to the presence of Ludovico, who was in the hands of a hairdresser, having the usual cosmetics applied to his long, soft locks, while another attendant trimmed and polished the nails of his hands. Sforza was dressed, all but the satin cassock which lay folded near by, while before him sat Almodoro, talking to beguile the last moments of the duke's toilet.

"Maledetto!" ejaculated Ludovico peevishly, as the name of his captain was announced, "he comes untimely: bid him wait until this business is ended, — or, stay, he must have weighty news; Almodoro, go you and speak with him; explain that I must forthwith to the Signoria; hear what he has to say, and hasten back; and, hark'ye, bid him keep under cover, or the sight of his face today will mar all."

And while the alchemist went on this errand, and while Ludovico ordered his guard of arquebusiers to be summoned, the concourse in the great hall increased, and talked more and more volubly, and groaned at the heat, and derided the bankers who came tardily. The place in which they were gathered had served, for over a century, as council room to the families of Visconti and Sforza, with whose portraits its walls were hung. The latter had succeeded so naturally to the extinct family, that, contrary to the practice of Italian government, the memorials of the previous line remained undisturbed. The only change had been made fifty years before by Duke Francesco, who, returning from a visit to Venice dazzled by the gorgeous effects of the Palace of the Doges, had enriched the Hall of the Signoria with tapestries and frescoes. At the head of the room was an enclosed space, separated from the audience, and here was Ludovico's chair, near which sat his brother, Cardinal Ascanio, the recipient of ostentatious and unctuous veneration from the prelates admitted to this precinct, and who, in olden days, were the nearest advisers of the Prince. Next in order were the nobles, seated in rows, behind whom, in a dense mass, stood the less favored.

It was precisely the hour appointed when a

door opened, and Ludovico entered, preceded by a group of pages: punctuality, he was wont to say, is a mark of education. Those who were seated rose as he entered, and he saluted the Signoria with ducal beretta raised from his head, and with a glance of his keen, earnest eyes. He was dressed without any of the insignia of his rank; a round cap with the crimson border turned up, an edge of frilled linen at the throat, an embroidered doublet, a sleeveless maroon cassock lined with yellow satin, black silk trunks and untanned shoes. He seated himself, intending to speak as it were from the throne; then, as moved by the excitement which gathered about this last attempt to redeem his waning glories, he rose and addressed to his listening subjects the appeal whose outline has been preserved by a contemporary.

He began by reviewing the beneficent features of his rule, or, as he punctiliously named it, his regency. He recalled the improvements and embellishments lavished upon Milan, and how men distinguished in science and art and letters had been attracted to it. "For," said he, "it has been my ambition to be remembered not only as a statesman, but more especially as a benefactor."

He passed to an explanation of the necessity which had been upon him of maintaining an armed force, of hiring soldiers from other countries, and hence of levying money. "I have sought," he said, "by being strong, to make our frontiers respected. It is the weak and wealthy who are the readiest objects of attack, and during my regency you have never seen the banners of a foe. If my administration has been costly, it has given you just laws, increased riches, and substantial peace. My evil fortune cannot be attributed to negligence or imprudence. These present reverses spring from the incapacity or the faithlessness of some on whom to my cost I relied. I have been deceived by masked visages. The harm can be remedied by our joint good will. The support of the Emperor Maximilian is promised; we need but patience and stout hearts, and in a few weeks a valiant army will relieve us. For myself, I declare that I have preferred the labors of government to any personal indulgence. What prince is there in Italy who has less abused his power? who has been so gentle and accessible to the humblest?"

He continued amid a faint murmur which could scarcely have been taken for applause.

"They cannot gainsay him," whispered Hermes, standing at the side of Bernardino Corte.

"No, but they cavil at heart; mark you how coldly they eye him. He should have flattered their vanity; as it is, the Signoria will listen and do nothing."

Perhaps Ludovico was already making similar

reflections, but he went on unruffled. He had little more than spoken these opening sentences when angry voices were heard at the entrance. Hermes left noiselessly by the private door, and discovered that the disturbance arose from Almodoro's attempt to enter after the delivery of his message to Sanseverino, and when the hall was filled and the duke's address commenced. The alchemist, perceiving the inconvenience his endeavor caused, would have withdrawn, but, as he turned, a man, against whom he jostled, assailed him with a torrent of abuse. When Hermes reached the scene, this personage was pouring forth a stream of invective such as only the volubility and the intensity of an Italian can sustain. His body quivered with rage, he had dashed his hat upon the ground, his arms cut the air with gestures, his hands now clenched, his fingers now extended in the speaking movements with which the Latins emphasize their words. Before him, pale, erect, silent, stood the alchemist, his tall figure drawn up, his face intent, a dangerous fire rising in his eyes. Pressing about them were the two or three score who had been unable to gain admittance. Suddenly Almodoro stepped forward, and, with a quick swinging movement of his right hand, dealt the other a heavy slap in the face.

In the confusion which followed, Hermes vainly strove to interpose between them. The throng increased, but as the law of Milan forbade the carrying of weapons within the city, the excited men who surged and clamored were without the means of inflicting very dangerous strokes. Hermes, feeling himself rudely pushed by some one elbowing his way backward, seized the new-comer violently, when, catching a glimpse of his face, he took him by the shoulders and dragged him clear of the crowd.

"There, Narvaez," he said with a laugh, as the fencer's angered features were revealed, "you are more obliged to me for bringing you out of that rabble than I am to you for trying to fracture my ribs. What a gorgeous figure! Per Bacco, where got you that silvery cape?"

The Spaniard had used a handful of the duke's gold to purchase an outfit of unusual richness, and, imitation being the sincerest flattery, Hermes smiled to see his own dress and ornaments reproduced,--the hair gathered in a net, the bracelets on the left wrist, the slashed doublet, the beretta with cluster of brilliants, the silk cloak shot with silver thread.

"You have a graceful way of walking through a crowd,--backward, with both elbows going," he continued.

"I meant to reach Messer Almodoro; hark'ye, padrone, I fear he may be hurt."

"And what concern is that of yours?"

"None, but it was a tempting quarrel; besides, within the door sits—you know whom I mean."

"Ha! I guess it,—the widow who is sworn to marry you whether or no,—am I right? And she gave you one amorous look, and you fled."

"Jesting aside, Almodoro is one against many, and delivered that stroke with a fervor I could not have surpassed. But he comes; see! they make place for him."

"Then let us move aside; we will walk as far as the piazza; you need have no further fear for the magician. Come with me."

"You know him well?"

"I know of him well."

"And can one believe the marvellous things told of his art?"

"No doubt, because they are vouched for to his discredit by the monsignori, and even by Cardinal Ascanio. His famous adventure with a siren rests upon their declaration, when charges were made before the Holy Office, so, of course, it must be true."

"I never heard of it. What did he with the siren?"

"There are some rocks in the sea near Amalfi called the Siren Islands, and famous since the days of Ulysses. If you sail about them, as I have done, you can see the bold face of the cliffs catching the flushes of dawn, and the waves dashing in and tossing the spray aloft like a banner. 'Tis there the sirens lurk far down in the deep sea caves, or bask in the sunshine on the water. Few ever got more than a distant peep at them, till Almodoro caught one and brought her alive to Milan."

"Mercy!" ejaculated the Spaniard; "with what bait should one cast for a mermaid?"

"You are right," answered Hermes, smiling at the fencer's earnestness, "that it required an extraordinary lure. These sirens already possess most of the things the black art can bestow,—perpetual youth, changeless beauty, fascination upon whoever sees them: the difficulty was to get within speaking distance; that gained, and one of them listening, Almodoro offered her the one faculty she had not—the gift to renew and rekindle the pleasures and memories and loves of the past."

"What could the wizard want with her?"

"To make her tell the future; for sirens can read events to come almost as well as sibyls. And, once in his power, he wrung from her all the secrets of the sea, and made her reveal the story of a thousand years to come. But it lasted only a few days; then the beautiful color the fair weather of ages had laid on her cheeks, and the violet green that her eyes had caught from the sparkling brine, faded, and she pined away."

"What! she died?"

"Yes, woman-like she craved the only thing impossible for her to possess."

"And that was —— ?"

"Almodoro's love: 'tis an odd story, but I meant not to waste so many minutes telling it. Come, let us walk faster."

"You will not stay and listen to the duke?"

"Why should I? he is not talking to me, nor to you either. Come, I have seen you but once since our return from Venice."

"Well, that was but a week ago, and doubtless you have been very busy since then."

"In these anxious days who has been idle?"

"Ah, but I mean busy with something the thought whereof makes the eyes glisten and the heart beat,—is it not rightly called Bianca Rucellai?"

"Beatissima! and do you, too, thrust gibes at me because I love a pretty woman?"

"Do you really love her?" inquired Narvaez, with interest grown suddenly serious.

"I do," replied the other earnestly. "I love her as she should be loved."

"But not enough to wed!" asked the fencer, turning upon him a face strangely flushed. "Remember," he continued, with a furtive, sidelong glance, "the lines of our Spanish rime, that love, like a lute, often needs fresh strings."

"And why not enough to wed? And what mat-

ter is it to you whom I wed? One would think
you had never loved a beautiful girl yourself."

"I never have," replied Narvaez, with an abstracted air.

"By my troth, I would no more be friends with
a youth who makes such an avowal, but that I
know you to be a hero. O Narvaez, it was sublime in you to take my place before the Star
Chamber!"

"Old Barbarigo bade me do so."

"But you risked your life."

"So he said."

"You did not slip a noose about your neck for
nothing. Now, what reward can I offer you?"

"Cannot one be generous without being thought
mercenary?"

"But you did it for me, who am no more to you
than yonder branch rustling in the sunlight."

"One would think you were trying to pick a
quarrel over it. Listen; since you must reward
me, I will have this or nothing. You shall tell me
what was in that odd triangular letter that so
worked upon the doge; surely, now that all is
over, it were no harm to tell!"

"You shall share the little I know about it, but
there may be eavesdroppers among these houses;
let us cross the piazza."

Passing down a street whose centre was divided
by an odorous gutter, they came to the Piazza

de' Mercanti, which had recently been cleared, and which, with other improvements, had so embellished the city that, in the popular phrase, Il Moro had changed Milan from a spinster to a fair maiden. Only one ancient building remained upon this square,— a tower ornamented at the top with stone busts of generals of a century before, which the designer had so pierced with apertures that the wind blowing through them on stormy nights made a dismal, whistling noise. They were a sorry group that had been so gallant in their prime, with here and there a nose or an ear or a chin missing, and all stained and weatherbeaten, and, on a boisterous night, moaning and shrilling their forlorn condition till the tower gained an evil repute. At another extremity of the piazza was a building, recently renovated, which was the palace of the Holy Inquisition, where heretics were tried, and blasphemers flogged, and Jews fined, and dealers in the black art racked. Above its terraced roof was a weather-vane in the form of a man, which Hermes remembered of old; for, as a child, he had often watched it at dusk from his nursery window, swerving in the breeze, and, to his boyish fancy, seeming a shape of ill omen. In later years his dislike of it increased, for when, at twilight, he beheld its misty figure veering above the shadowy roof-tops, it seemed to his imagination possessed of satanic intelligence, and pointing, with fiendish humor, at the follies and failures of his life.

"You ask me about that mysterious letter," resumed Hermes thoughtfully. "From something the duke said, it must have contained an allusion to some sorceries of the doge's which bind him yet. Old men like Barbarigo are great favorites with witches; they will cackle when they catch one, like poor people laughing at a rich man's joke."

"But how could the duke know of Barbarigo's sorceries?"

"Doubtless from Almodoro. He is a Venetian and as old as a church; perhaps he was implicated, and, now that he is my uncle's soothsayer, may have furnished a useful hint."

"And was it for such wanton trifles we were sent on that mad adventure?"

"At least I stipulated a splendid reward. Can you keep a secret? I bargained that the duchess and Francesco be released, and that their captivity end: I have done my utmost; what sad fate awaits them I know not, but at least they are free."

"That was bravely done, and like you; but a week has passed and they are still in the castle?"

"They could not be turned adrift at an hour's notice, but in a day or two I shall persuade Isabelle to ——"

Hermes paused involuntarily as a sudden expression of unconscious repugnance appeared upon

Narvaez' face; and, turning to seek its cause, he beheld the alchemist following, with gaze fixed intently upon them, and with an amused expression as he perceived the concern his appearance produced.

"Pardon me," he said suavely to Hermes, "if I have come unwittingly upon your confidences; but blame me not, for the streets are free to all, and you should not blurt strange tidings."

"You have the reputation," answered Hermes bitterly, "of surprising many secrets; but you shall rue this meeting if you betray what you have overheard!"

"Rue this meeting!" repeated the alchemist with sneering imitation; "what must I understand from such harsh words?"

"That the will gains upon me to run you through the body, and to end at once your eavesdropping and your wizard's tricks."

"I am unarmed." answered Almodoro gravely, "as the law commands all honest citizens to be. You bear a rapier through that exemption which extends to an officer. But swords are committed to the duke's captains for nobler uses than that you contemplate. A day's ride from here are twenty thousand enemies of your family; but lately there was an encounter with them; were you there to draw upon an armed foe the blade with which you threaten me?"

Before Hermes could answer this taunt with the defiance that sprang to his lips, the soothsayer waved him back.

"Since this release is Ludovico's pleasure," he said, "what care I further? As for you, Sforza, since you are thus eager for blood, be on your guard at the next Ottobrata, for one shall cross your path then who will do you a mischief. And at Christmas think of me, and remember the proverb, '*Wings come quickly to unguarded treasure.*'" Then, casting a searching look upon Narvaez, he added:

"Bold youth, I have no weapon, but I will smite you with a whisper—a syllable in your ear."

Hermes, watching the alchemist as he moved to the side of Narvaez, saw the fencer reel back before the faint words as though before some direful stroke. Then Almodoro laughed softly, and said aloud to Narvaez, who stood gazing speechless upon him:

"The truth peeps from your eyes—it always does for me."

The Spaniard labored under such intense distress that Hermes, regarding Almodoro no further, stepped to his side, and, taking him about the shoulder, said:

"Heed him not, man, but pluck up a brave heart; and look! he goes away; therefore be comforted. In truth he has a ready wit, and if his sword be as keen as his tongue—— but what was it he whispered?"

"Ask me not," answered the fencer faintly, gazing with a relieved expression after the retreating figure : "that strange being is no man that reads in people's thoughts!"

"As a friend, I beseech you, confide in me the words that so strangely startled you."

"There are things which cannot be told."

"So you, too, have a secret?"

"Alas, yes. I may tell it you on my deathbed, but never before."

CHAPTER X.

LAGO LARIO.

Three days after Sforza's fruitless appeal to the Signoria, a travelling retinue of unusual proportions was collected at daybreak in the courtyard of the castle. There were horses for the duke and his companions, mules for the servants and baggage, and the chargers of a score of knights who were to escort Ludovico in the flight which the advance of the French and the disaffected state of his capital rendered necessary. His last resource was now to seek assistance from abroad, and he was about to depart silently, so that, before the Milanese divined his purpose, he should be hastening from among them.

The preceding day had been devoted to calculating the resources of the castle against the siege it must presently sustain, and in visiting the ramparts which were being made ready for defence: in good and valiant Bernardino Corte's hands it was to endure as a pivot for operations when the duke should return with a host of Swiss mercenaries. Into it were collected eighteen hundred cannon of various shapes and sizes, a year's provisions for three thousand men, and in the great keep were stored the jewels and part of the treasure. To the governor's fealty all this was confided with the charge, "Defend it as you would your own for four months; if within that time you are hard pressed and I come not, you may make terms." To which injunction Bernardino answered with vehement protestation that, while his life continued, the castle should not yield to less than an enemy swarming in over demolished ramparts.

Among those assembled were Hermes, equipped to the gauntlets for the journey to Innsbrück, and Narvaez, who had come to report to his patron. They had supped together the previous evening, but, the intended flight being a military secret, Hermes, at parting, had merely bidden his companion come at dawn, and so Narvaez, wrapped in a white cloak, arrived betimes, and wondered at the groups and the caparisoned horses, and the knights stamping and fault-finding as their armor was buckled on, and the files of men hastening to the treasure-keep and back, bringing small barrels of ducats.

And as Narvaez, standing by a great pile of stone cannon-balls, watched and listened, Hermes appeared and tapped him on the shoulder.

"You see," he began, "it was for a leave-taking I bade you."

"I divined it," replied the fencer; "and now I cannot shake off a premonition that, if we part, it will be to meet no more."

"That is last night's Barolo," replied Hermes, laughing; then, changing his bantering tone to one of sadness, he added, "you are to await my return; for during this absence you can render me a favor I shall always value."

"Say not so, dear Hermes, illustrissimo, but take me with you; I served well enough once before to be trusted now."

"Alas, this is to be an absence of months, with long days on horseback, and you are not famous as a rider."

"How dreadful it will be in Milan! A foreign army, no fencing, and you gone. The days will be more sombre than an old man's dream; and as for me, I shall grow as melancholy as a caged bird to which no one speaks."

"You have the widow to turn to."

"I will set her at the French."

"In truth I feel sorry for you, but vastly more so for myself, thus chased forth—perhaps forever." Then, catching the Spaniard's hands, he added: "If you think of me sometimes, remember only the pleasant days we have spent together—the tourneys and races we have watched - the Sunday afternoons at Monza—ah me, Narvaez, a flight like this makes one think that if we knew beforehand the disappointments of the future, hardly a man would care to live!"

"Oh, take me with you," pleaded the fencer beseechingly; "you know I mind no hardship, and we shall comfort one another in exile."

"It cannot be, for there is an infinite service you must render me here in Milan. I have confided to you that I love a beautiful girl: I have not told you how artless she is, how trustful, how untaught by the lessons of the world; if she remain here through all these calamitous days——"

The request that was to follow died on Hermes' lips, as, to his astonishment, Narvaez grew livid with anger, and, without another word, turned on his heel and walked rapidly away. Before Hermes had recovered from his surprise, his uncle called him.

Ludovico spoke in quick, earnest words. "The moment has come," he said, "when I must transfer Isabelle and Francesco to your care, whether they will or no; set them free, commit them to the French, or lead them to some remote province: it is yours to decide." Then, beckoning the governor, who was feverishly urging on the preparations, he desired him to summon the duchess.

"Here, in the cortile, before all these men!" objected the governor, aghast at his master's command.

"And why not?" retorted the duke; "do prisoners no longer come when bidden, or is not this courtyard good enough to set her free?"

"Free!" echoed the other, whose usually ready intelligence seemed stunned behind his disconcerted visage; then, recovering himself with an effort, he bowed and hastened away.

But he went no further than the guard-room at the entrance of the building in which Isabelle had been secluded, and here he threw himself upon a bench and fell into a tremulous cogitation.

The duchess had been released by him at dusk on the previous evening, and was now far on her way to meet the French, her boy remaining in Bernardino's quarters while she made this early overture for the surrender of the unconquerable castle. The little Francesco was guaranty that, at her restoration, the governor's good offices should be rewarded. For two days Bernardino had been in frequent converse with the duke, and, through all the instructions given him, no word had been spoken of Galeazzo's widow. He had assumed that she would be left in his custody, and that the haste and preoccupation of Ludovico's departure would prevent a final interview. At Isabelle's entreaty, and upon her insistence that they must be beforehand with their proposal, he had braved the risk and set her free. And now the prisoner must be instantly produced, at the alternative of exposure.

In that age of action and of sanguinary emergencies, men reached determinations promptly. The governor sprang up the stairway to the vacant apartment, and, locking its heavy doors, tossed the key away. Then, hurrying to his own quarters, he found there a lieutenant of the guard and half a dozen arquebusiers. He called the officer aside, with a grim smile at the chance which brought that particular man on duty.

"Cola," he began, "I have but one minute to speak; shall I use that minute to make your fortune?"

"Si, signore," replied the lieutenant, with a sinister twinkle of the eyes.

"Promise your men a hundred ducats apiece if the work is well done. For yourself a thousand, and that vacant captaincy we spoke of."

"Si, signore."

"You are to do precisely what I tell you, and be deaf, dumb, and blind to all beside."

"Si, signore."

"I shall enter this courtyard presently with one person, perhaps with several. If I fold my arms thus, the portcullis must be lowered; if I drop my handkerchief, you and your fellows are to run to me—and mind, Cola, there are to be no wounded—it must be neatly done."

"Si, signore."

"It matters not who the persons may be, even were one of them the duke himself."

"But, signore!"

"Tush! I must away. When all is done, you shall choose yourself a sweetheart."

When Bernardino returned to the presence of the duke, he found Ludovico bidding good-by to his two little boys, whom their uncle Ascanio was about to conduct to a refuge in Germany. The cardinal had put off his habitual robes and also his usual suavity. Had his advice been followed, a douceur would have been paid the French as their "damages." But the high treasurer Landriano had scoffed at this, and now the French were upon them, and all was lost. And likewise he had objected to the appointment of Bernardino Corte to so supreme a trust as the command of the castle; but Bernardino had been chosen despite his protest, and so the cardinal was vexed, and answered in monosyllables when his brother addressed him.

And as Ludovico stood chatting with his boys, he noticed the waiting governor, and saw that he had returned without Isabelle, and then his sombre brow grew darker as he asked:

"Why have you not brought the duchess, as I bade you?"

"Because," answered the governor with profound deference, "she refuses to come."

At this extraordinary declaration the cardinal laughed sardonically, while Almodoro gazed in amazement at the speaker, and even the guards looked up from their work. Then Sforza asked angrily:

"Did not you command her in my name?"

"I did; but at this early hour she has not yet risen: moreover the door was locked, and she refused to open it."

"And how is it that you leave to a prisoner the means to lock herself in and thus defy you?"

"I did so in obedience to your own order, that, apart from the daily inspection, the duchess be at liberty to seclude herself."

"Then call an armorer to beat in that door upon the instant—quick! an armorer and a couple of men."

The cardinal, who stood listening, grew merry over this discourse, and chuckled as he said:

"It will be a lengthy process breaking in your jail doors, and, ere you return, I and the children will be on our way: see, it is almost sunrise, and we have but twelve hours' start of the French."

"The French! a leprosy upon them!" retorted Ludovico. "Yet stay, Ascanio, I would have a moment with you—some other must look to this woman—Hermes, it shall be you—you begged the witch's release, go and deal with her as you will."

Hermes lost no time in availing himself of this

permission: followed by Bernardino Corte, he started in the direction of the building the duchess had occupied. It would have fared ill with him had he passed out of view of his companions, for at his heels walked Bernardino with hand laid upon the ready poniard; but the quick eye of Hermes noticed the open shutters of Isabelle's rooms. He halted abruptly, turned a suspicious glance toward his comrade, observed the governor's right hand instinctively tightening upon his stiletto, then, with a backward step, he brought the heavy rapier within reach. At this the governor made an odd grimace, and threw his hands aloft in vehement remonstrance, and poured forth a torrent of reproach.

Did the friend who had been his boon companion suspect him? and, if so, of what? And otherwise, what meant this strange menace? why scowled he thus? and why stood he ready to draw upon one who extended the grasp of fellowship?

To all which Hermes answered impatiently: "Those shades have not been closed since yesterday; the duchess is no longer there where is she?"

The governor cast aside as useless the denial that rose to his lips. He reflected in that brief pause that his life was now at stake, that a few minutes must be gained, that Hermes must be coaxed fifty paces further, just out of sight of those in the

court. He answered, therefore, without hesitation:
"I intended, as soon as we were beyond the reach of observers, to tell you the dreadful secret, that the duchess escaped with her child last night."

"Escaped! none ever before escaped from this castle. Speak me the truth—you have killed her! Oh, cruel-hearted!—was it by the duke's command, or does it hide some greater infamy of your own?"

At another time Bernardino would have been quick to resent such words, but he had now a more sinister purpose than the usual appeal to weapons, and he mastered his anger and answered:

"These are harsh words, Hermes, but they are uttered in hasty misunderstanding, and you will recall them when I tell you all."

"Tell it then quickly, ere I summon the guard."

A vindictive flush passed over the governor's face at this threat as he replied, with a smile: "Come with me and I will do more than tell; I will prove the truth."

"How will you prove it?"

"Through those who discovered her flight, and who, at my order, made vigorous pursuit, only to learn at a late hour that the fugitives were still miles ahead on the road to Pavia."

"And where am I to hear this tale?"

"At my own quarters."

"And thence to the bottom of an oubliette.

Look you, Bernardino, of all this you shall clear yourself upon the instant and before the duke."

The governor folded his arms in silence. And as he did so the air was filled with the clamor of a throng outside the castle. At the sound Hermes sprang back to the entrance, and, as he passed the gate, the portcullis fell behind him. He divined at a glance what had happened. The departure of Cardinal Ascanio and the Sforza boys had attracted a great crowd, and when Ludovico sallied forth with his attendants and the train of pack mules, a cry arose that the city was abandoned to the enemy, and his progress was opposed with staves and stones till, at Sanseverino's command, the knights laid lance in rest and charged, opening a broad avenue, upon which they left here and there a lacerated body, pierced, and trampled by the horses. The news flew, and from far and near men came running with savage cries. For twenty years the Milanese had grumbled at Ludovico's presence; now they cursed his flight. Their own apathy was forgotten, and they would fain have presented their usurper in chains to the French. But Sforza heeded not, as, with a wave of the hand, he urged his followers towards the highway: then he called to the people:

"Forbear bloodshed; you will have sorrows enough ere long;" and, borrowing from a homely proverb, he cried, with a defiant gesture:

"The King of France has come to dine with me, but it is with you that he shall stay to sup."

The cavalcade started afresh, while the escort wheeled and covered its departure. A mile beyond the walls the duke halted and allowed his followers to gain some distance; then, dismounting, he approached a tablet which stood in a cluster of willows overlooking the river. It marked the grave of Beatrice; here had been her favorite walk to and fro across the grass and the wild flowers; often she had sat in meditation upon a fallen oak, whose trunk still lay half in shade and half in flickering sunlight, and here, beneath the familiar shelter, and in the place which, in life, had been her accustomed retreat, she had asked to be buried. Ludovico remembered how once he had accompanied her to this spot, and how, through her girlish ways and jesting humor, she had disclosed strange and startling ambitions, inciting him to dazzling ventures and taunting him with timidity, and saying, as she tossed the jessamines at her bodice into the Olona:

"See how idly fine resolves drift upon a sluggish current!"

And now he was there alone, and time had made sad havoc with their jessamines. In that place each humble object before him, the associations that sprang to remembrance, and even the thousand inanimate voices of nature,—all spoke of the faithful and valiant heart that was at rest. He bent with infinite tenderness, and kissed the stone on which his dead wife's name was carved; then, as he mounted the horse that Almodoro held, the alchemist whispered a word of encouragement.

"It is all a fool's trick," muttered the duke, as they rode forward. "Have you, who spend your days in the scrutiny of strange things, ever found a queerer puzzle than the ups and downs of the world? I often think there is a malevolent force —all ages have called it by the name of some divinity—that baffles our hopes, and mocks at our sorrows, and bewilders the future. But look, they beckon us, let us on; time presses and we have far to go."

They trotted ahead as fast as the treasure-mules could be urged. In the crisp October morning the broad rice-fields mellowed to yellow stubble, and the creepers that the first chill of autumn had touched, hung in crimson garlands along the russet hedges. Here and there, among stately poplars, were farm-houses with thatched roofs that, afar, resembled the pointed haystacks on the horizon. At intervals along the leafless forest a cypress stood like a sombre shadow, while, in the misty distance, the crooked olive-trees raised their branches in tints of silver grey. The air was still, but for an occasional hum of insect life, and so clear that, as they advanced, the faint white outline of the Alps became brilliant and glistening. They approached Como by a road skirted with villas and gardens such as the Italian imagines, with ancient statues, and shady alleys, and shrubs curiously trimmed to the semblance of centaurs and dragons. The long straight walks were strewn with tiny twigs and leaves of last summer, and were stained in places with a dark green mould. There was the soft splash of water trickling from huge, mossy vases, and here and there, through a break in the foliage, struck an arrowy shaft of sunlight. Upon all rested an atmosphere of delicious repose, of high-bred antiquity, as though successive generations had delighted to touch the lanes and arbors and parterres with taste and refinement, and to people the solitudes of cool, deep shade with marble images of poesy.

Half an hour later three large, square-sailed barges bore Ludovico and his companions and his treasure out of sight of the little port, with its array of pink and lemon Venetian blinds, and, along the quay, the tables of the venders, and, in their midst, three sculptured Apostles, whose gaze was wistfully fixed across the water, as they raised their broken and lichen-grown fingers in benediction. Swiftly impelled by the long oars of the boatmen, they steered across the bends and expanses of the lake, whose glassy surface reflected the rocks, the overleaning foliage, and the sun-flushed crags in rich, deep coloring of marble tints.

On lofty points stood vine-grown towers, while in the distance appeared the Alps, touched in the sunlight with opalescent hues. At the prow sat Ludovico and Hermes and Almodoro, gazing on the motionless tranquillity of the scene before them, and heedless, for the hour, of the perils and difficulties to come. Hermes had more than once traversed the lake, and he knew the names of the picturesque villages, with their quaint belfries and arcades, and fishing-skiffs moored in the shallows, where the water turned from sapphire to glistening emerald. His reverie strayed from the sheltered orange gardens to the olive groves, and thence, by imagined forest paths, to the solitudes above. Often in boyhood had he listened, at the twilight hour, to his nurse's fireside tales of Lario — of the village where she lived, of the castle on the heights, of romances and feats of arms, and how, on fine afternoons, the hawks circled tirelessly in the heavens; and there, yonder, was the castle, now ruined, its fragments embowered in myrtle, and above it a sheaf of feathery clouds, and a pair of hawks soaring and wheeling against the blue. And there came back to him a quaint remembrance of this same old and garrulous nurse, as he saw, at the water's edge, the great rock where her elder sister was drowned half a century ago, when they were girls together. Then, to her childish fancy, as she often said, the few years between them were a vast interval, and her playmate had been mentor as well. But when she reached the cares of middle life, and reverted to the holidays of her youth, it seemed a younger rather than an elder sister she had lost; and, as the years went by, the dead girl's memory became ever relatively younger, until, looking back from her infirmities, she remembered her only as a happy and care-free child.

Then he thought of Bianca Rucellai, and bewitched his fancy with the picture of the villa he would build for her some day. It should stand upon one of those headlands, with the purpling hills before, and the chirp of birds in the air, and on many a summer's morning they should walk together through the laburnum groves, and delight to lose their way and find their love anew. Now and again the duke and Almodoro talked softly, and once a contadino, wondering at the unusual apparition, saluted them with a halloo that reverberated from the opposite cliff. The amber brightness of afternoon faded to the violet of dusk, and a lethargy stole upon the scene, as though the curtains of the evening had been drawn. Far away rose a thread of smoke, and presently lights glimmered, and they neared Bellagio, "the place of pleasant repose," bordering the lake in a dim, gray mass. At length the duke turned to Hermes, and, breaking the spell which had fallen upon them all, asked abruptly, as one who returns to an unwelcome thought:

"And the duchess; you gave her freedom? Wherefore was that freak that she would not speak with me?"

"Uncle," answered the younger Sforza, with bitter reproach in his voice, "it is to small purpose that I tell you what you already know—that the duchess was no longer in the castle: whether liberated by Bernardino, or put to death by him, I cannot say."

Then a look of consternation came over Ludovico as a terrible suspicion seized him. And when, two weeks later, the news was brought that the impregnable stronghold had been yielded for a price which a sarcasm of the enemy stipulated should be paid out of the treasure it contained, he cried aloud (so says the chronicler):

"Verily, since Judas there has been no baser traitor than Bernardino Corte!"

CHAPTER XI.

FESTA DELL' OTTOBRATA.

SIX weeks had elapsed since the duke's abandonment of his capital, and while the French occupation proved costly and harassing to the Milanese, it did not bring the grievous inflictions they apprehended. The susceptible populace had been vastly impressed by the numbers of the French; by their weapons, whose peculiarities added to their formidable appearance; by the gorgeous pageant of the court; by the calm and resolute aspect of the king. In Louis' train as, he rode to the ducal residence in the castle, were Ives d'Allègre and Cardinal Amboise, and, among many others, two youths destined to become famous,—one, an Italian, the son of Pope Alexander, commonly called Cesare Borgia, but now styling himself by his recently acquired French title, Le Duc de Valentinois; the other, Pierre du Terrail, better known by a sobriquet he had taken from the red castle in which he was born,—Le Chevalier Bayard.

When the first overture for capitulation was made, the French showed themselves liberal in promises, agreeing with Isabelle that she should be restored to power, and with Bernardino that, in addition to half the treasure in his custody, he should receive the highest honors of France. Whatever expectation may have remained that the fugitive prince would return to tempt again the fortune of arms was extinguished when the castle surrendered, and its garrison marched out before the eyes of the astounded Italians and amid the gibes of the French. So fatal a weakness, or so vast a betrayal, surpassed comprehension.

On the last Sunday of October was to be observed the poetic Festa dell' Ottobrata, a holiday when, in former centuries in Italy, the townsfolk went out into the country to look upon the mellow tints of autumn, to walk in the vineyards and taste the purple grapes, and to breathe the fragrance that filled the air with odors finer than the flavor of wine. It was a festival of pagan significance, with the archaic dances and garlanded processions of harvest and vintage. And on this day the myths of antiquity recovered a momentary influence; the old, romantic delight in nature rekindled; the forest was beautiful as when trodden by the silver-sandalled huntress; and across many a meadow, where the wild flowers saluted their feet, went the laughing girls and youths of sylvan days.

Early in the afternoon of the Ottobrata, Valentino and Le Bayard were seated in the room which had formerly served as Ludovico's antechamber, having dined with the officers of the king's household at the usual hour of mid-day. On the morrow they were to be separated; for Borgia, with a corps of French and Swiss, was to march to that conquest of Romagna which was to be the first page in his military life; during the weeks they had passed together on the journey from Paris and in the engagements before Asti, so warm a friendship had united them that they had bound themselves by that ancient pledge of chivalry which was the comradeship in arms of one knight with another. Both had just reached the age of twenty-three. Le Bayard was thin and small, with pale, shaven face, and severe, refined features, and deep-set eyes that were filled with animation. He was nervous in manner, given to quick, incisive gesture, and possessed of great muscular strength. His companion was of larger and more powerful build. His countenance was stronger in expression, owing to the high cheek-bones, the aquiline nose, the steady, unflinching gaze. He wore his hair gathered in a Spanish net, and his face was covered with a silky auburn beard. Upon the French youth's ascetic visage rested the inspired look of one whose ideal is of unselfish service, of unsullied duty. In Valentino's meditative, self-confident mien one divined the adventurous soldier aspiring to more tangible possessions than an illuminated fame. Borgia's life was consistently vicious, while Le Bayard's only passion was a mystic liaison such as the morality of the sixteenth century condoned. At an early age he had been fascinated by a famous beauty, Yolande de Fruzasco, the young wife of a Count of Savoy: in the brief acquaintance of their first and only meetings they loved—but their fault was no more than a spiritual attachment. Le Bayard was wont to declare that there is nothing so ennobling as a disappointed amour, and, however this opinion may have been improved upon, it is certain that he remained constant through lifelong separation; until his death it was their habit, once a year, to send to one another some trifling remembrance, but they met no more. Only the memory of those youthful and ardent meetings remained to Le Bayard, to become transfigured in the afterglow, and to be so cherished and exalted that, as he himself declared, it became the inspiration and treasure of his life.

They had just entered the room, and the winetaster who, with a page, had brought in a flagon, was performing the function of his office in emptying a cup before their eyes; Le Bayard seated himself as he cast an admiring glance upon the heavy Turkish rug with which the floor was spread.

"Foi de mon âme!" he exclaimed, "how delicate a texture; I know nothing so soft to the foot, unless it be the mossy paths of Dauphiné."

"Soft to the foot! ay, so it is," assented Valentino, filling two silver goblets, "and sweet to the taste is this wine, and more to the purpose. Let us drink, and your walks shall seem to you like ways to the celestial gardens."

"I love not these wines of Montserrat," answered Le Bayard with a wry face as he sipped; "they leave a resinous taste upon the lips."

"Some day we will drink a fiasco together in Rome—would we were there now to pass this Ottobrata falconing on the Campania in view of the violet hills,—and to-night,—bethink you of this night beside the Tiber—the dreamy music, the starlight reverie, the ruddy torches and lanterns reflected in the water, the glimpse of beautiful women—the women with their black, glossy hair twisted in fantastic coils, their great, lustrous, brown eyes, their necks bared, or half covered with a crimson kerchief: do you know, Picquet, they found such a one in marble a year ago beneath some ancient rubbish—a wood nymph, the Venetian ambassador declared, carved in the days of the Cæsars, and the very image of one of our Campania girls. All Rome went to see her—the rabble, the learned, the soldiers, the priests—more than all, the priests, for she was nude—and as I stood looking at that superb, lithe, sinewy form, and studied the half-divine, half-sensuous beauty of her marble face, I thought how many generations of men had looked upon her with an amorous passion, how perhaps for ages to come she will inspire that same mute yet eloquent worship that greeted her as she stepped forth from the ruins of antiquity—but tush! I remember, Picquet, you care no more for our women than you do for our wine."

"No; but I would give a month of life in exchange for a day in Rome. And it is said that from the Alban hills one can look upon the sea— how I should love to look upon the sea!—for they say there sparkles upon it a thread of sunlight that carries one back to boyhood; have you ever beheld the sunlight sparkle on the sea, Cesare?"

"Yes; and this morning I saw it sparkle in the eyes of a girl, a daughter of the banker Rucellai; I have wooed her in vain for weeks, but to-night, at the ball, we dance a Moresca together. A Spanish fencer named Narvaez, with whom I practice, first told me of her, declaring her the prettiest maid in Milan, and saying that were he king of France he would carry her back with him to Paris."

"A truce to your talk about women! It may be long before we meet again; it was last summer that we first met—how long ago that seems, and to-morrow you leave us."

"But only for a few months."

"You take a corps of our best troops, D'Aubigny told me."

"I laughed myself to sleep last night thinking of the scattering there will presently be among the signorotti of Romagna."

"For so ambitious a man," observed Le Bayard, "I think you were at fault to abandon the Church. With the help of the king you might have succeeded your father."

"The Church," repeated Valentino meditatively, "yes, sometimes I regret it. To live outwardly under the greatest of all restraints, and at the same time to be habitually in emotional relations with—ah me! who could wish a happier life than that of confessor?"

"This Sforza, whom we have driven off, would have made a better than you. Amboise told me his private life rarely held a fault."

"He is a singular mixture of weakness and strength. He will yet come back with a swarm of mountaineers to fight you."

"D'Aubigny will trample them like straw."

"Your D'Aubigny takes things too easily. Some day he will be caught like a boar that has eaten a paunchful of acorns, and lies asleep in the sun."

"Ha!" laughed Le Bayard, "there speaks the Italian. But the knights of France will not be asleep, and they——"

"And there," retorted Valentino, "speaks the

Frenchman. But no doubt you are right. The lanzknechts cannot meet you away from their defiles, and it would not surprise me if Sforza were taken."

"I should like to see him—that is, to meet him in battle, and then bring him into our camp."

"Your camp is not large enough to hold all who will presently cross blades with you," answered Borgia, piqued at the unconscious disparagement with which his companion often referred to Italians. "These Swiss you scatter so readily left Charles the Bold and half his Frenchmen dead on the field; and when you confront the Spanish phalanx, which I have watched drilling and marching at Naples, you will find it steady as a palisade, and worse than a lighted petard to lay hands on."

"Mordi!" ejaculated Le Bayard with animation, and unwittingly forecasting his own end, "how gladly should one take the gift of death from such a foe! But hark, some one comes; it must be Cardinal Amboise," he added, rising to salute his Eminence.

Valentino remained seated. He cared little for cardinals: had he not been a cardinal himself?

The door opened to admit the diminutive figure of a page; Le Bayard muttered a curse at his needless punctilio, and Borgia smiled.

"My masters," said the boy, "his Majesty desires your presence."

At this summons both took their caps and followed. They were the attendants of honor of Louis, his companions often in the field, or at table, or for an hour's chat when the day's task was done. Valentino was interesting to the French king for his graphic descriptions of Italian politics, and of the intrigues of the Spanish viceroy at Naples. It was not, however, for relaxation that they were now bidden. In Ludovico's former library they found the king seated in the capacious leather chair which, though worn and shabby, was infinitely comfortable, and which association had made a favorite with the departed duke. Before him was a large table spread with parchments, and furnished with the meagre writing materials then in use. Among these was a paper-weight which Almodoro had given to his patron; it was a slender crystal stalactite, and the wise man, knowing the years required for the formation of each hair's-breadth of its length, had measured the centuries upon it, and marked a few famous dates with a spiral silver branch. An inch back from the point was notched the last Crusade, a finger's breadth behind followed the name of Mahomet, then came Rome destroyed, and a little higher the Christian Era; after an interval was Hannibal, then Marathon, and then after a space the Golden Age, and still further Moses — the Pyramids—Babylon; beyond this, the stone had formerly extended several inches, or, as Almodoro computed, twenty thousand years; but one day Cardinal Ascanio, with a malediction upon the wizard and his calculations, cast it from an open window.

Louis was carelessly dressed in a fleur-de-lys embroidered cassock, which much use had faded and made threadbare. He looked weary and ill-humored. Despite his easy conquest of Milan, Italy was proving as troublesome to him as to Charles the Eighth. His generals complained of the Swiss; the Swiss grumbled at everything; the Venetian alliance was found to be but a name; the outcast Sforza was raising an army; the Spaniards held menacing language from Naples; his regiments were decimated by what the soldiers called the Italian malady.

At one side of the room two clerks stood before a wooden dresser, counting gold coin. If Ludovico had failed to obtain a voluntary loan from the Milanese, his successor had drawn from them an unwilling contribution of no mean proportions. Sequins and ducats, almost unalloyed, and struck in large, thin pieces, made no unmusical sound as they were dropped in heaps; and although this noise had continued monotonously all the morning, the king found in it no discordant or disturbing accompaniment to his labor. He scarcely raised his eyes as Le Bayard and Valentino entered and saluted him, so busy was he writing with a long swan's quill, that made a loud scratching upon the parchment, and with which he was tracing line after line of heavy black characters, whose illegibility attested the French monarch an indifferent penman. After an interval a door opposite the king's chair was opened, and one of the captains of his military household appeared, followed by the ex-governor of the castle, Bernardino Corte. The appearance of this personage had changed considerably in the company of his new friends. His face was pale, his eyes bloodshot and haggard, his dress neglected, his expression that of one who has learned how vain may be the promise of a prince. He bowed to the king, and glanced in recognition towards the young officers. Louis looked at him fixedly, without answering his salutation; Valentino returned a cold stare; Le Bayard averted his eyes, and Bernardino's white face became overspread with a deep flush. There was a moment's silence, broken within by the chink of the gold pieces, and without by a murmur of the harlequin's games wherewith the French thought to emulate the Italian Ottobrata.

The king pushed his writing back upon the table, settled himself comfortably in his easy chair, stroked his hair down over his brow with one hand, while with the other he toyed with a bunch of keys that hung at his girdle.

"Messer Bernardino," he began, "I have granted this audience in deference to your urgent desire, although, frankly, I knew not that we had further subject for discourse. And if I have constrained my inclination, it is not in recognition of services you may have rendered, for they were to be compensated in a manner agreed upon, and the price has been paid. But in a few days I leave Milan; this is our last interview; therefore I am disposed to listen to whatever it may be your will to say."

These cold words smote the heart of the renegade, and for a moment his utterance failed; then, with an effort, and with the eyes of all fixed attentively upon him, he said:

"Maestà, it is no new matter that I would speak of. It was not for a bribe," he exclaimed, looking about from one to another, "that I delivered this castle. Its surrender was the completion of an earnest and patriotic design. It was transferred to you as a military necessity, but only upon the promise that it should revert to the duchess Isabelle." Then his voice faltered as he added: "Through the long last year of her captivity she and I watched the times together, and in the flight of the usurper we read the opportunity for her restoration to her own. Your faith was pledged that you made war only upon Ludovico, yet after all these weeks she waits in vain, while

I am hindered from seeing her, and deprived of the child she confided to my care, and even refused admission to your presence. O King," he sobbed, in a voice hushed almost to a whisper, "is this the honor of France?"

Louis controlled a movement of impatience at this blunt speech, and asked:

"How can the affairs of the duchess concern you, or by what authority do you presume to speak for her?"

"Sire, I have more than once declared to you our love."

The king struck the table violently with his hand.

"Bernardino Corte!" he exclaimed, "you fill yourself with vain and senseless dreams. Think you that the Duchess of Milan would wed with you —a mere soldier of fortune?"

A firm and complacent assurance appeared upon the countenance of Bernardino in place of the tremulous anger with which he had first spoken. Then, with the simple conviction of one for whom no doubts exist, he replied:

"Would that she were here to answer for herself!"

"And would that content you—to hear her speak her mind freely?"

"It is not I that need to be thus assured, but you; let me but meet her eyes with mine, and you shall hear her renew the pledge which gave me all the sweetness of earth."

"By the Holy Grail, this favor you shall have," answered the king with sarcastic emphasis; "only, as it might embarrass the candor of the lady's declaration if you were standing by, you shall withdraw into the adjoining room—a tapestry covers the entrance—you will hear as plainly as you hear me now."

"But after that?" inquired Bernardino, warned by some prophetic instinct, "what avails it me to hear the duchess pledge her faith if afterwards I am restrained, as I have been all these weeks, from seeing her?"

The king eyed him quizzically as he again toyed with the bunch of keys which, in his nervous moods, it was his habit to swing from side to side. "Rest assured, good Bernardino," he answered, "you will be satisfied; but mark me, speak not, nor give the slightest sign that you are near, nor let your joy wring from you so much as a murmur—else beware!' And the king motioned Borgia and Bernardino to the adjoining room, while Le Bayard was sent to invite the duchess to his presence.

Isabelle entered the room a few moments later, ushered in with ceremonious courtesy, and received by the king with an affectation of debonnair good humor. Her handsome face had acquired a care-worn look in place of the haughty resignation of her captivity. All hopes of recovering the duchy had faded before the evasions of the French. Even her boy Francesco had not been restored to her, nor had she seen him since the night he was left with Bernardino while she fled to Pavia. He had passed to the custody of a French officer, while she was left unheeded, save for the clamorous letters and messages of Bernardino.

The king drew forward a chair for her, and placed himself with his back to his writing-table, against which he leaned; mindful who was listening, he at once directed his interrogatory to the subject in which Bernardino was concerned.

"I have sent for you," he began abruptly, "because it is necessary to conclude a question upon which we have touched heretofore. You have repeatedly urged your claim to Milan, and insisted upon the advantages that would result from your rule. It appears that upon these particulars you had a covenant with the officer who made over this castle to me. Is it not so?"

"Sire," answered the duchess with painful emotion, "you will hold a helpless woman but lightly answerable for what she says or promises in escaping from a cruel imprisonment."

"But it is nevertheless true that you had entered into an agreement with your jailer."

"It is true."

"He asserts that you made him a solemn promise of marriage."

"If that be a promise which despair yields to the edge of the sword."

"But Bernardino Corte maintains that you freely pledged him your love; that you would wed him now, were you both at liberty."

"I have explained and answered this to you before."

"Nay, but, for the love you bear him, answer it now."

"O king, mock me not in my misery, else may God render it to you again!" And Isabelle bowed her face in her hands, while Louis stood silent a moment in involuntary compassion.

"Suppose I restore you Milan if you wed Bernardino," resumed the king, "will you take it and him together?"

At this cruel taunt Isabelle rose to her feet, and, with face aflame, flew to her besetting idea.

"Do you not know the crime which links that man with my sorrow?" she asked. "Have you not heard that it was he who poisoned my husband, and cannot you understand the infamy of being loved by him? Can nothing make you feel for me the shame of his advances, the humiliation of his pity, the scourge of his pursuit, the loathing with which I yielded to his conditions?—oh, does not the thought of so bitter an anguish touch even the heart of a king?"

The French monarch and Isabelle confronted one another in silence,—he calm and sardonic, she trembling with excitement and the restraint of tears.

The clerks desisted from their work an instant, and from the piazza came the faint noise of drums and merry-making pipes.

"Then must I tell him," pursued Louis, unmoved, "that you refuse to see him again."

"Strike me off his head for the dullest rogue that ever betrayed his trust!" ejaculated the duchess.

"And your boy Francesco?" asked the king, unable longer to resist the prompting of his malicious nature.

"You have promised, day after day, to restore him to me; let this, at least, be realized, and the rest may go."

"It was but yesterday Cardinal Amboise spoke of him and said: '*Let not the wolf cub escape, or ten years hence he will return to vex us.*'"

"How can an outcast and beggared prince disturb the king of France? Give him to me, and I will take him far hence to Bari; we shall neither of us ask to see Milan ever again."

"I have anticipated your thought of placing him at a distance, but with this difference, that it is best that henceforward his abode be in France."

"Sire, I am powerless to dispute with you; give him to me, and together we will journey to some secluded place beyond the Alps and live together."

"That you may train him the while to the mystery and silence of Italian ways; that you may fill his mind with ambitions, and his heart with hate of me. No; you must be separated. I have bestowed upon him the abbaye of Nourmentiers; there he will forget his unhappy country, he will exchange the name of Sforza for one the Church will select; instead of condottieri chiefs he will have godly brothers for companions; he will learn to resemble the last drone of them all—what ails you? why so pale? You dread the pangs of leave-taking; nay, fear not, I have spared you this trial, he is already far hence, he has been gone four days; and for yourself—you spoke of Bari, well, nothing hinders your going there at once!"

"Inhuman!" shrieked the duchess, in a paroxysm of fury. "So long as breath remains to me will I pray that you be followed by the sting of my curse, that the cries of your wounded and the faces of your dead may haunt you and blight your days!"

The king's lips contracted and his hands clenched, but before he could answer there came from the adjoining room the voice of Bernardino Corte, speaking inarticulately, gasping; a heavy crash followed, then all was still.

Louis sprang to the door and threw aside the tapestry, and beheld Ludovico's faithless lieutenant stretched on the floor, his own stiletto plunged into his heart. And above him, with right hand uplifted, stood Valentino, silent and motionless, gazing fixedly down upon the bleeding and inanimate form.

CHAPTER XII.

LE CHEVALIER BAYARD.

The military faults which caused the discomfiture of Charles the Eighth in Italy were repeated by his successor, and with the same results The French forces were distributed along several lines of operations, and when the outcast duke suddenly reappeared at Como with sixteen thousand Swiss, he found Louis returned to Paris, Ives d'Allègre campaigning in Romagna, and not half the French army available for a battle. Perceiving his enemy's weakness, Ludovico marched upon Milan and entered it before the absent regiments could be recalled.

But if the re-occupation of his capital was thus lightly effected, the French continued in undisputed possession of the castle, and the duke was constrained to lodge in a palace on the piazza, and to distribute his officers in its vicinity. Among the few billeted under the same roof with him was his nephew, Hermes Sforza. The return of this youth had been less joyous than he had anticipated, for, upon presenting himself at the Palazzo Rucellai, he had found that magnificent pile deserted, and had learned with difficulty from a timorous custode that his sweetheart had fled a month before with a cavalier named — the speaker recalled his name with difficulty — ah, yes, it came back to him now — Valentino ; and her father, — poor man! the sainted Madonna alone knew whither he had followed them. Then Hermes covered his face with both hands and wept, and remembered the warning of Almodoro.

The day following, while moodily pacing the streets, which had lost their familiar animation, he bethought him of the fencing-master, and straightway found Narvaez unemployed, living upon the sequins which had rewarded his zeal at Venice, greatly scandalized at the vicinity of the French, — whom, as a good Spaniard, he detested, — and weary of idleness. Whatever qualms of conscience he may have felt at sight of his former patron, whose confidence he had betrayed, were perfectly dissimulated. His first words were of admiration of the beard which Hermes had allowed to grow during his four months' absence. His next were of the *suicide* (for so the French proclaimed it) of Bernardino Corte. It occurred to the unsuspecting Hermes to engage him as his personal follower for the campaign, after the manner of officers of distinction, who frequently enlisted a fencer in their retinue, with whom to cross swords for pastime, and who, in emergency, was more than a looker-on. His proposal was instantly accepted upon the attractions of good pay, a servant, and horses.

If Narvaez resented the presence of the French, he expressed himself still more forcibly at the aspect of the army of lanzknechts which Ludovico encamped on the outskirts of Milan. No such ill-favored troops had appeared in Italy since the descents of Saracenic fleets some centuries before. Such was the levity of the Italian populace, that they marvelled like children at the strange costumes and uncouth manners and rude weapons of these mercenary mountaineers, of whose prowess and ferocity so much had been said.

They were formed in battalions, each bearing a flag emblazoned with the emblem of its canton: the bear of the Oberland, the bull of Uri, the fish of Lucerne. Their costumes were of various shapes and colors; all wore jerkins of cloth or leather, long, tight, striped breeches, reaching from the waist to the ankle, and fitting within heavy untanned shoes; their helmets were of leather, furnished with brass rims, and profusely studded with nails. The officers were distinguished by iron casques decorated with coarse plumes, and those whose rank entitled them to a horse wore soft boots falling in folds below the knee. For weapons, some were armed with long, jagged halberds, others with an axe and cross-bow slung at the shoulder; all had either a sheathless sword, or a bare, thick dagger stuck through a thong at their belt. The most remarkable feature in the entire array was the number of women, many of whom carried infants, while others were followed by children old enough to walk; all bore immense burdens, containing provisions, cooking utensils, and extra clothing for their consorts in the ranks. Some had chickens perched upon the bundles they shouldered, while others were attended by fierce dogs. Such were the "Lansquenettes," as they came to be called, probably the most suffering and miserable of their sex in any age.

Early one morning, a week after his return to Milan, Hermes was summoned to Ludovico's room. As he passed through the antechamber, the pages and attendants who, without undressing, slept at night upon tables or benches, rose drowsily before him. He found Il Moro seated in profound thought before a manuscript map, which he scanned with occasional reference to a roll of reports. Between the windows blazed a bright fire of pine logs, for the February air was damp and cold; above it projected a great chimney-piece carved with the temptation of Eden,—Adam at one side, Eve at the other, and between them a spreading tree, wherein the arch-serpent had coiled, and whence he gazed, as though in mockery, with outstretched tongue.

The duke laid aside his despatches as Hermes entered, and, motioning to a seat, was about to address him, when he observed the lugubrious expression of his face.

"Peste!" he exclaimed, "are you still brooding about that baggage of a runaway Rucellai? You have had a disappointment? You will have a dozen more in the next few years. Philosophy tells you that through life the things that be, are merely the counterfeit presentment of the things that might have been. Does not that bring a solace to your soul?"

"My uncle," answered the young man, "you would not jest thus if you had ever felt——"

"Love, you are about to say," interrupted the elder Sforza. "Listen. I seldom speak of it, least of all to the young; but you will find it true that some men seek to gather the love of their life when it is premature; others wait till it is over-ripe and has fallen to the ground, then with might and main they shake the tree; but the bitterest fate is his who mistakes a weed for a flower, and plants that in his heart."

"I shall ne'er give over till I see that man's blood on my sword, and in *her* face the crimson of shame."

"Be that as you list," replied the duke carelessly. "In the mean time I have summoned you for an expedition of importance."

"Not another visit to Venice?"

"No. This time an inspection of the outposts on the highway to Pavia. Take with you an escort of twenty or thirty men——"

"Twenty or thirty men galloping about the outposts would rouse the whole French army. One that I have will suffice."

"I warrant, the same knave that got you and himself and Barbarigo into such a quandary. Yes? I thought so. Then put him upon the worst horse you can find, and, if the enemy appear, clap in the spurs yourself, and away, and perhaps you may be quit of your precious escort. Here is a written order, and a map of the way; gather all possible information along the front, and be back before the Ave Maria. We march to-morrow at break of day."

An hour later Hermes, accompanied by Narvaez, rode out towards the chief outpost of Ludovico's German cavalry. The sun had risen ere they mounted, and now cast a feeble brightness upon the desolate fields whence the peasants had fled and the cattle had been driven away. The only sign of life was, upon the stubble, a company of hungry crows, which, at the approach of the riders, filled the air with their cawing, and flapped their way swiftly out of sight. But presently they perceived that the outpost which was to be the first stage of their journey had already received a visit of an animated nature.

Upon the retreat of the French from Milan, the Chevalier Bayard had received permission to serve with the rear-guard, now nearest to the enemy. Observing the isolated situation of the detachment which formed the Italian van, and which numbered only three hundred, he resolved to attack it with the fifty troopers he commanded, augmented by half a dozen cavaliers to whom he proposed the adventure. The intended surprise failed, for the Germans were found with their armor on and their horses harnessed, and, at the appearance of the French, sounded a bugle blast and set upon them. The disparity of one to six delighted the eccentric genius of Le Bayard, and he galloped his little band into the midst of the enemy with so fierce an onset that the German centre gave way. The flanks of their line wheeled in, however, and dealt so many and such vigorous blows that, but for the prowess of Le Bayard and his companions, upon whose superb armor the German blades made little impression, the result would have been the reverse of that the French had designed. Before the din of this conflict reached his ears, Hermes beheld the cloud of dust which the trampling of so many horses raised, and which floated over the combatants. And drawing near, and hearing the war cries, and beholding the *mêlée*, he unsheathed his sword and put spurs to his horse. Narvaez, who bestrode a less fiery charger, dropped behind. Their approach attracted sidelong glances from such of the combatants as had leisure to divert their eyes, for they might be the forerunners of a weighty reinforcement. Le Bayard, however, when once well entered upon a hearty exchange of blows, cared nothing for reinforcements, and, furious that Frenchmen should be held in check and buffeted by a foe he despised, he shouted to his comrades, as they loved France and valued the favor of fair women, to follow. Then, casting aside his sword, which he had broken, he grasped a mace which hung at his saddle bow, and whose weight was about four pounds, wherewith he dealt such ponderous strokes that the lanzknechts fled from his path. This retrograde movement instantly became a general flight, and Hermes was swept away by the rush of the fugitives. With such hot haste did the Germans ride, that Le Bayard, who led the chase, could only come up with two of them, and to each of these he administered a blow which sent him reeling from his saddle. The like must have befallen Narvaez, whose steed lagged, and who was little accustomed to horsemanship, had not his indifferent mount, and the unskilled way in which he rode, attracted the notice of the bravest and gentlest of men: in the instant of raising his formidable weapon, he lowered it in silence and dashed by.

It was not long before such a headlong gallop brought him in sight of Milan, all unconscious that his companions had drawn bridle, and that he was now alone in the pursuit of two hundred. At a bend in the highway he beheld the familiar battlements, the lowered drawbridge, the sentries on the walls, attracted by the fugitive cavalcade, whom they discerned, even at that distance, to be of their army. Right before him dashed the lanzknechts, raising a cloud of dust that veiled the road behind from the wardens who gazed in search of the enemy before whom they fled in such suggestive disarray. The sight overtempted Le Bayard's military discretion, and, supposing himself to be followed at least by some of his comrades, and to be able to gratify himself with the triumph of seizing one of the gates of Milan, he plunged across the bridge, which was immediately lifted behind him. He saw at a glance the desperate nature of his position, and measured at a thought the dishonor of surrendering his arms. A single chance remained, which was to cross the city and escape by some gate on the opposite side, where no alarm could yet have been communicated. But before him crowded a hundred of the lanzknechts, who had turned about as soon as the drawbridge was raised, and from the ramparts came whizzing a crossbow shaft that glanced from his helmet, and half a dozen stones slung by hand, which fell with heavy thuds upon the ground. He brandished aloft the mace which had done such redoubtable service, and, shouting his battle-cry, "France! France!" dashed into the thick of the lanzknechts.

And now arose the din of a singularly disproportioned conflict. It was heard even on the piazza, and faintly reached the room in which Ludovico still sat before his map, measuring marches and distances. Nearer and nearer it drew, till the duke, startled at the extraordinary tumult, sprang to a window, and there beheld the spectacle of a French officer, encased in beautiful armor, riding a wounded and exhausted horse, dealing furious blows at the score of men who crowded upon him from out a press that impotently yelled and gesticulated. He was silent now,—too hard-pressed and desperate to spend breath in war cries. The duke scanned him curiously. His helmet had lost its plumes, at his side hung an empty scabbard, and on his breastplate was engraved Our Lady of Sorrows. While some showered blows upon him, others flung handfuls of dust against his closed visor, to blind him through the sights. Suddenly his great bay horse plunged violently and fell to the ground, when both were overwhelmed by the lanzknechts, who tore off the horse's accoutrements, and wrenched the mace from the hand which now relaxed in token of surrender.

As Le Bayard rose painfully to his feet, the captain of the German Horse claimed him, and led him away. Ludovico, looking from his window, followed him with his eyes, and, wondering at the chance which had brought an enemy single-handed into their midst, ordered that the German captain be summoned. The messenger had been gone but a moment when Hermes appeared, and recounted the rout of the outpost he had been commissioned to visit, dilating upon the extraordinary prowess of the stranger they had just seen disarmed, and upon his rare magnanimity in sparing the life of the defenceless Narvaez; whereupon the duke modified his order, and desired that the prisoner be brought before him.

An hour later he was ushered into Ludovico's presence, being announced by the name which he had given, Pierre du Terrail,—a name, of course, unknown, as his achievement of the morning was his first encounter. In the interval following his capture he had made two requests,—that he be allowed to bathe himself with water, and be given a bowl of bread and milk to eat. Having been thus frugally refreshed, he was conducted to the duke.

Sforza received him alone. The young Frenchman bowed gravely as the door closed upon him, and remained standing with eyes fixed upon the dark, beautiful face of his enemy, whose appearance, and the fame of whose dramatic life, were familiar in the French camp. Sforza's gaze rested with a not unkindly interest upon the spare figure and pale, ascetic face. It was a meeting in which Italian historians of that knightly period delight.

Le Bayard was clad in the close-fitting buffalo-skin doublet and breeches worn under a suit of mail. About his neck was a reliquary, the first gift of Yolande de Fruzasco, and from his shoulders depended a long white cloak which had been rolled behind his saddle. His hands hung down before him, carelessly clasped together; the thick brown hair was brushed half an inch down over his forehead, and fell at each side of his face in long straight locks. The duke remained seated at the table at which he had been writing, and, pointing to a chair, addressed him in French.

"Be seated, Monsieur le Chevalier," he said; "you must be weary after such violent exertion:" then, as Le Bayard took the place indicated, he added, "I have sent for you to look more closely upon so valorous a soldier, and to ask the motive of your strange assault. Was it through an accident that you entered Milan, or did you think to storm the city single handed?"

Le Bayard listened with an air of curious expectation to these first words. On being told that he was to be taken to the duke's presence, he had wondered what could be required of him, and now an amused smile came to his lips as he answered.

"Monseigneur, I, with a few others whom the king has honored with his service, had yet to merit this favor by some prowess of arms; and, being stationed with the rear-guard over against Milan, we were minded to charge an outpost which lay before the gate, and, becoming heated with the engagement which ensued, I followed across the bridge, unconscious that I was alone."

Sforza observed him attentively as he spoke, and remarked the dignified composure, and the curt, matter-of-fact way in which so gallant an exploit was described, and with a half-quizzical, half-incredulous look he replied:

"Your blood must indeed have been hot to plunge thus into the midst of a city filled with men at arms."

"Par la foi de mon âme!" answered Le Bayard, with a Gallic shrug, "Monseigneur must be equally sensible of the charm of danger, or he would not be here."

"Forsooth!" ejaculated Sforza, piqued at the words, "you have set me a good example, and King Louis shall find that a man who stands before his own, will show as great daring as strangers in search of adventure. But I sent for you in kindness, to ask you about yourself and the school of arms in which you learned to fight one against an hundred; to offer you refreshment—here at the word it comes,"—and the duke motioned a servant who had entered the room to advance, and to place upon a table a tray he carried, whereon were little gilt rolls usually served to royalty, a crystal saucer of olives, and a Venetian flagon encased in silver filigree, through which could be discerned the words,

> Health, Wealth, and Honor be his,
> Who drinks from a pure and moderate cup.

A wine-taster who had followed the domestic stepped forward, and, filling a goblet held ready in his hand, drained it at a draught; this done he filled two glasses which stood on the tray, bowed to his master, and withdrew. It was a wine whose clear amber color attracted the eye, and whose flavor and bouquet possessed so soothing an influence, and produced so genial an exhilaration, that, in the vineyard, it was known as "*the wine of good humor.*"

"Will you drink?" asked Ludovico, when they were again alone.

Le Bayard rarely used wine, for stimulants were contrary to his habit; but to refuse would seem to hide a misgiving which the sinister repute of Italian princes might have suggested. He therefore raised the glass to his lips, and emptied it with the Milanese salutation "Felicità."

"Answer me a question," resumed Ludovico, balancing his glass, in which the wine of good humor sparkled like a topaz in the firelight; "are there many in the French camp equal to such feats as this you count so lightly?"

"I am the youngest and least experienced of them all."

"But you have seen military service?"

"Pardon me, this is my first campaign."

"Then in what cunning school of arms were you apprenticed?"

"In the school of a hardy and abstemious youth. My father served the king until enfeebled by age, and from him my brothers and I learned the use of weapons, and such sports and exercises as become a soldier, and, further, to read a little, and to write our names, and to know the same again when written. I spent my days in the air, among men, and thereby escaped the vanities with which the children of the rich cumber and exhaust themselves, and which it takes half a lifetime to cast off."

"Tell me something of your home. Do you live in a city?"

"I have spent most of my life at our Château de Bayard. My first boyish recollection is of being put on a pony and taught to tilt with a rod at a wooden figure fixed in the ground, which was called 'l'Anglais.' My delight was in long rides, especially in spring, or in the early autumn, when a golden flush falls on our hillsides in Dauphiné. And in winter I scoured the forests for game, and loved each day as well as the brighter afternoons of summer; for you know, Monseigneur, that in France there is something cheerful even in a winter's morning, as though a little of the September brightness remained."

"Merely riding and hunting makes a dull life," observed Ludovico, interested in the odd character of his visitor. "Did your father never take you to court?"

"Our fortune is too scant for courts or journeyings," answered Le Bayard, without hesitation; "only, when a tourney was proclaimed at some neighboring city, he took my brothers and me thither, and hired us suits of armor and bade us lay on."

"He must be a tough-fibred veteran, this father of yours."

"He trains us after the manner of his own bringing up, whose maxim is written on the flyleaf of our Bible, that nothing purifies the spirit like suffering, and that the grandest things in life are done under adversity."

"I, for one, should differ with the fly-leaf of your Bible, and say that the best efforts are those kindled by love. You will find it so some day when you marry."

"That must remain a lesson unread by me."

"And why?"

"Because I have taken a vow of lifelong celibacy."

"But a time will come when you can no longer ride fiery steeds, and deal hurts, and smite the stranger. And when old age steals upon you, will it not be a sombre life to look back upon—no love, no children, no pleasure, no solace?"

The French cavalier answered slowly, yet with the fervor of a young crusader.

"So few," he said, "reach the age whereof you warn me, that I give it small heed. But, standing now between youth and maturity, my purpose is so to serve the king that, when my vigor is past, my conscience may pronounce me worthy to kiss the earthly sepulchre of Christ. Think you that after that I could ever be unhappy in the retrospect?"

"You talk like a sage, and you fight like the knights we read of; alas, they are not many nowadays."

"I shall not be thus commended by my superiors; I may even be severely punished."

"Punished! and how do the French punish one another's deeds of valor?"

"My folly may be rebuked by ordering me to

the rear on the day when we have the honor to meet you in the field."

"You have a great thirst for the giving and getting of blows," rejoined Ludovico; "but," he added, "do you imagine that so redoubtable an enemy will be released, now that fortune has put you in our hands?"

"I have already agreed with the captain whose prisoner I am; he consents to release me, with my horse and armor, for a thousand ducats, and that sum will be paid from the French camp to-morrow."

The duke's interest had passed from curiosity to an admiration he did not seek to conceal.

"God forbid," he said abruptly and with emotion, "that so valiant a soldier should be detained for the sake of a purse of gold. I will pay your ransom myself; you are at liberty to return at once to your comrades; and if this adventure bring you to the presence of the king, say that I charged you to salute him in my name."

Le Bayard sprang to his feet, his pale face suddenly aglow with delight at the magnanimous spirit which released him. He took the duke's hand, and would have saluted it with the courtly reverence of that ceremonious age. But Ludovico checked him, and, drawing from his finger a ring, gave it him and bade him God-speed, and caused his horse and armor to be brought.

And twenty-three years after, when *le chevalier sans peur et sans reproche* lay dying upon an unfortunate battlefield, he pressed to his lips the reliquary of Yolande de Fruzasco with the passionate despair of one who dwells, in death, upon remembered kisses; then his gaze turned from the strange faces of the Spaniards who crowded about, and rested, it is said, upon the ring of Ludovico Sforza, as though its sight recalled some rare and chivalric memory, worthy to be cherished even in the last moment of life.

CHAPTER XIII.

THE MONASTERY OF DIVINE LOVE.

THE advance from Milan was unobstructed until Ludovico approached Vigevano, where, while preparing for the assault, the Swiss stipulated that they be permitted to pillage the town. But when the scaling-ladders were ready, and the drums about to beat, the duke's heart smote him, for Vigevano was his birthplace, and he interposed before his hirelings, promising them a ducat apiece, at which the disappointed mountaineers vented their anger in imprecations.

This was repeated at Novara. By pledging the sack of that city he obtained untiring efforts, and, such was their appetite for the reward, that breaches were presently effected, through which they poured with irresistible violence, and forthwith began plundering the houses, torturing the women, and butchering whoever resisted. Horror-struck at the sight, Sforza again interfered, and bivouacked his savage auxiliaries between the city and the position to which the enemy had withdrawn. It was at the peril of his own life that he thus plucked their prey a second time from them, nor was their loss forgiven.

To a busy afternoon in the bivouac before Novara had succeeded a stormy evening. At sunset a mist rose from the rice-fields, and the clouds grew heavier with every hour. The raindrops hung in the hemlock branches until an occasional stir sent them pattering down. Before Sforza's tent crackled a fire whereon a servant made ready to grill some mutton bones, and, near by, a table had been spread with bread and cheese and flagons of wine.

The duke lay within, asleep on a camp bed. In the doorway sat Sanseverino, the general of his forces, muffled in a cloak, and with his head bound in a cloth through which a little blood had oozed, and at his feet rested an empty straw-covered fiasco. Near by, half recumbent under a blanket, was Almodoro, with eyes fixed upon the fire as it sent showers of sparks into the murky darkness. In their search for firewood the servants had brought from the edge of a neighboring millpond the débris of a skiff whose planks had for years been alternately soaked in water and dried in the sun. When tossed upon the blaze of forest branches, these fragments emitted an odor as sweet as oriental spice, and their flame brightened with prismatic tints until, beneath the alchemist's brooding gaze, their lurid embers seemed touched by some unholy incantation. At a few yards' distance, two wet and hungry-looking sentries leaned against the trunk of an oak, with their halberds resting between their hands; on either side was the encampment of the army, and behind, in a low, sombre mass, lay the city of Novara, difficult to distinguish, save where a lofty glimmer indicated a watch-tower on the rampart.

Presently the duke awakened, and the servant was withdrawing from the coals the supper he had cooked, when two figures emerged from the darkness, and, passing the sentries unchallenged, came within the firelight. The first was Hermes, and the other a Swiss courier who declared himself the bearer of an important despatch from Sforza's diplomatic agent at Berne.

Upon hearing this the duke came forward, Almodoro and Sanseverino roused themselves, and the grilled bones were forgotten. Ludovico took the letter, then, beckoning the others to follow, he returned into the tent, where, by the light of a lantern, he read it first to himself, then softly to the others as they bent eagerly forward. It was a curt warning that the Helvetian Diet had passed an edict recalling from Italy all the Swiss troops serving on both sides.

Three blank countenances met Sforza's as he looked up aghast from the parchment. Almodoro was the first to speak.

"This is bad news," he said, "but it cannot be a surprise, for it has long been impending. That Swiss should slaughter Swiss, in a foreign quarrel, seems folly to the Diet as well as to the soldiers."

Ludovico turned from him with the impatience of a man who finds little comfort in the uncompromising truth. "Think you we could continue the fight," he asked, addressing Sanseverino, "were all the Swiss in Lombardy on their way to the Alps?"

"No," immediately replied that officer; "there are four Frenchmen in Louis' camp to one Italian in ours."

"And," pursued the duke, thoughtfully, "it were hopeless to tempt the Swiss to continue with us after this edict reaches them."

Sanseverino laughed bitterly at the question, then checked himself with a grimace of pain, and raised his hand to his wound. "You may well say so," he answered; "with the discontent that prevails, and the furtive parleyings at the outposts, such a command would sheath every lanzknecht blade."

"But," objected Almodoro, "the Swiss of King Louis are the regular levies of cantons, whereas ours are enrolled as volunteers, and are not subject to the orders of the Diet."

The commander-in-chief shook his damaged head moodily, but vouchsafed no reply.

"What think you, Almodoro?" asked the duke. "With troops that will not fight, and Time that will not wait——"

The alchemist interposed with quick, decisive speech.

"Grant me this hour!" he exclaimed vehemently, with a sudden inspiration, "and if you have wit to profit by what I shall do, all our troubles shall be ended within four days."

"You rave!" ejaculated Sanseverino, with angry impatience. "You think to sit here and work charms while——"

But Ludovico interrupted his lieutenant with a peremptory gesture, and turning to the soothsayer, at whose last words he had caught, and speaking with the breathless interest of one who fears to have good tidings taken from him, he bade that worthy explain himself. Thus admonished, Almodoro unrolled a map, and, tracing the road from Novara to Bellinzona, said:

"The edict will obviously be sent by two messengers, one to each camp; and they will come by this route, for it is the direct road, and shorter by a day than any other. From the terms of your letter, the courier who bore it had two days' start of those the Diet was about to send. Now, suppose the letter destined for our camp miscarried; imagine that its bearer fell into evil hands, while the other pursued his way; would it not result that the Swiss in the employ of the French would forthwith march off?"

"But these rogues of ours would go with them," objected Sanseverino. "The vedettes speak together daily, and such a mandate would be known in one camp almost as soon as in the other, and would be equally obeyed in both."

"I began by saying," retorted Almodoro, "that something would remain for you to do; your charge, from this moment, is to prevent further communication between the camps. Put the Italian cavalry on guard outside our lines; when Louis' Swiss march, your men may hesitate; then offer them the plunder of the enemy, guaranteed by hostages, and fall upon the French, ten to one, and destroy them."

"As I live, it is worth trying!" cried Hermes, who had listened with delight.

"Yes; but, like many ingenious plans, it takes much for granted. Where would you meet these messengers, or how identify them, or how distinguish one from the other, or how escape the dangers that would attend every mile of your way? Behold the road; it runs in rear of the enemy. You would be made prisoner, and might think yourself fortunate if you escaped the fate of a spy."

"'Tis true; and true it is that these are timid doubts of yours. Do not I offer to render you this service? Have I asked that any other shall share its peril? I only say we touch the supreme instant when everything is at stake; when I, for one, am ready for any sacrifice."

"And if you fail?"

"You would be little worse off than now."

"He will not fail," ejaculated Hermes, "and if he can forgive my rudeness on a bygone day, I will go with him and share every danger—and dangers are lessened when divided."

"I thank you," replied Almodoro, not unkindly; "but I shall do as well, or better, alone."

"I beseech you, refuse me not," insisted Hermes; "at some moment I might serve you to advantage, if only with a pair of keen eyes."

"It may not be amiss," assented Almodoro, reflectively, "and bring with you the nimble swordsman — the youth with whom I met you walking."

"He is a brave fellow, and has followed me before to my profit."

The alchemist smiled in silence.

"You start at once?" queried Ludovico.

"Yes, upon the instant; by midnight I shall have circled past the enemy's camp, and thence on till sunrise."

They took a hasty leave, Hermes casting regretful eyes towards the savory mutton bones. Ten minutes elapsed before he returned with the fencer, who evinced a lively aversion to the company of Almodoro. Then their horses were brought, and in a moment they were out of sight.

Before they had ridden half a mile the quick-eared Narvaez called a halt.

"Something approaches," he said, listening intently as they drew bridle. It was a murmur of voices—the voices of men singing, and the tramp of hundreds of feet. At sight of the glitter of torches Narvaez guessed its meaning, and led the way a few yards within cover of the trees.

It was one of Sforza's regiments, which, having lingered upon some temporary service, had marched through the evening to rejoin the main body, and was now lighting the way and beguiling the distance. Nearer the singing came, and at times all joined in a chorus, through which floated the jödel echo, associated then, and for centuries before, with the Alps. The head of the column came in view amid the glare of torches, and the long files trudged after. At intervals the lansquenettes passed in twos and threes, and these only, beneath their heavy burdens, sang not. Now and again went by a cluster of lanterns, preceding a couple of officers, and by their light could be seen the fantastic costumes, the bearded faces, the bedraggled plumes, the long cloaks, the halberds with fanged and glittering blades. Last of all came a dozen footsore laggards, and, mounted upon donkeys, three drowsy friars, the spiritual guides of the battalion.

Towards midnight Almodoro and his escort emerged upon the highway, the branches swaying in weird figures as the alchemist led on in silence. He alone was unarmed, Hermes being provided with a pair of pistols, then a formidable novelty, and the fencer with a short blunderbuss, which could scatter death amid a troop of horse. When the morning light revealed their road stretching between lines of poplars and disappearing in the gorge of a defile, Narvaez, who was unaccustomed to riding, begged that they might turn aside into some woods whence a rivulet issued. While their horses browsed they breakfasted upon bread and mortadella, which Hermes had thrust into the saddlebag at the moment of departure. As they rode forward, the sun appeared and dried their clothes. Towards noon Almodoro unrolled a map and indicated their whereabouts, pointing to a cross which Narvaez surmised to signify a graveyard, but which the alchemist informed them marked a famous resting-place,—Il Monastero del Divino Amore. This monastic hostelry, he said, stood in a fork of the northern routes, and, there being no shelter south of it, and to the northward only the wild spurs of the Alps, whoever passed that way must needs seek its hospitality.

Five miles further Hermes spied a turret, and presently they perceived a castellated building. Their approach was signalled by the barking of shaggy dogs, which bounded furiously out, but wagged their bushy tails as the visitors came upon them. When they drew rein, the oaken entrance was seen to be open. It was studded and braced like the portal of a fortress, but, amid these indications of its former character, was nailed a crucifix that betokened its conversion to a spiritual stronghold. The outworks had been demolished, the chains by which the drawbridge was raised had disappeared, the wooden scaffoldings which protected the rampart had served for firewood, and the ancient loopholes had been enlarged to windows. Over the way was a stable and a blacksmith's shop, where a cheerful sound of hammering went on, and when the fencer beat upon the door, a couple of unkempt contadini ran out, while at the iron-barred casement of a porter's lodge appeared a chubby-faced sacristan, peering down in curious scrutiny. His observation proving satisfactory, he addressed them with a formality which delighted the Spanish heart of Narvaez, asking what their commands might be, and, on learning their needs, desiring them to leave their horses opposite, and then to enter the courtyard, where he would be waiting. When they had done this, he shook each gravely by the hand, imitating the mellow voice of the Italian prelate and the air of one who blesses the universe, as he begged them to follow to an arbor, where they might converse during the few minutes that remained till the mid-day meal was served.

He added, as they crossed the court, that this happened to be "razor day," and jestingly pointed to a window, through which, in passing, the last half dozen friars were seen being shaved and freshly tonsured. They noticed, too, in the corner of the sacristy in which this operation was performed, a waxen figure of the divine Bambino, equipped with tinsel and trinkets, whose interposition had worked miraculous cures, and from whose presence within their walls the monks drew unspeakable comfort on stormy nights, when the wind blew and the devil whistled and groaned through the tree-tops, while they lay awake listening in the dreadful dark.

In reply to a stream of questions, Almodoro declared himself and his companions to be a patrol from the French camp, sent to meet two Swiss couriers, who were to be hourly looked for.

The sacristan, having extracted such further particulars as to their names and histories as the alchemist thought proper to give, vouchsafed the information that this was, in very deed, the Monastery of Divine Love; that a century ago it had been a fortress; that in its present more blessed state it was under the protection of the Virgin, in testimony whereof the brothers numbered thirty at the time the abandoned castle was made over to them, and now, after the death of all the original members, behold they still numbered thirty, all in good militant order save himself, who was growing fat, and the superior, who was grown sad ever since,—but that was a long, long story, and must wait a season of greater leisure.

And when the bell rang he led them to a fountain that rippled over from a marble basin whose original whiteness was lost beneath a deposit of mould. Here, at their guide's suggestion, our horsemen washed their hands, this being the only opportunity for ablution. Upon entering the refectory they were received by the superior, a man whose ascetic face reflected something of the austere gravity of cloister walks, and whose soft accent declared him a Venetian. Unlike the sacristan, he asked no questions, merely saying that they would find the fare simple, but that, such as it was, they were welcome.

At sight of him, and at the sound of his voice, Hermes' heart almost stood still an instant; for he recognized the eccentric fugitive to whose care Barbarigo's brother had confided him in Venice, and whose strange story had moved him in that anxious hour. But the superior's glance showed no answering recognition. Doubtless change of dress and the growth of beard in the last three months' campaigning had altered Hermes' appearance.

The refectory was furnished with long tables and benches without backs. From the black rafters hung a candelabrum made of two short boards nailed crosswise one upon the other, with a candle stuck in each of the four ends; the rope whereby this contrivance was raised or lowered being attached to the wall. At intervals between the long lines of tin plates and mugs were wooden salt-cellars, bowls of dandelion salad, and fiaschi of vinegar-tasting wine. During the repast, which was served steaming hot in two courses, no one spoke, for all were required to listen to a discourse which a brother read. And each, at rising, bowed to the superior and walked out, the friars to return to their cells, and Almodoro and his companions to look to their horses.

After an inspection of the stable they strolled along the highway, and Hermes, after deliberating with himself, resolved to make no mention to his companions of his previous meeting with the superior. The latter had clearly forgotten him, and fear of his possible recognition would only perplex and complicate their plans.

"Maestro," said Narvaez, addressing Almodoro, "are you content to rest upon it that the Swiss will halt at this place? May not they," he added, with thoughts evidently reverting to the Moors of his Andalusian sierras, "stop here merely to water their horses or to change them?"

"No man," replied the alchemist, "whose occupation it is to carry despatches, could make his horses last if he used them so severely; as for a re-mount, you noticed that all those in the stalls are common field ponies. Now, there being no station south of this before Novara, and none north of it for forty miles, we may presume that they would leave their last resting-place so as to arrive here at sunset: hence I look for them late in the afternoon to-day, or to-morrow."

"Were it not wise," pursued the fencer, who, in the intense interest which absorbed every other feeling, seemed to have forgotten his antipathy to Almodoro, "to inquire of the stable men the usage of couriers,—whether they rest here the night; whether spare horses are furnished; whether perchance two are presently expected?"

"It were well done, and to you I allot it; and, while there, note minutely the doors and windows, and the access from the rear. Meanwhile, Signor Hermes, if you are disposed to oblige me, you will find again the talkative sacristan, and get from him everything about the rules and ways of the monastery. And while you are both thus well employed, I will skirt the building and learn if there be a subterranean passage. We will meet hereabouts within an hour, and bear in mind to keep your weapons always ready."

Before the appointed time had passed, they were again together, and, in answer to an inquiring glance, Narvaez said:

"The stable men declare that couriers pass here frequently, and that it is their practice to rest the night."

"And I," said Hermes, "found the fat sacristan fresh from his own private table, looking rosy and contented, and smelling of onions. He smacked his lips and told of fasts and vigils and retreats, and then he entered upon the story of the superior—how he was the last of a Venetian family that had given a doge to the State, and that, at the command of the Council, he had left the cloister to wed his cousin, that their name might not perish. And after he had lived some years with her, and she had borne him two sons, he quietly vanished one day from his familiar places and returned to the life he preferred—of poverty for the glory of God."

Then said Almodoro: "I have found three private ways out of the monastery: one by a postern at the rear; a second through a door that leads into a dry moat, but which has been so long unused that nothing short of a battering-ram could open it; the third by a steep path into the valley. Moreover, I learn that we are to sleep on pallet beds in the refectory, which will answer perfectly, for we shall be together, and near the great gate, if at any time we need to get our horses. More than this we cannot yet determine."

"I have wondered all the morning," said Hermes, with diffident hesitation, "that you do not resort to the powers of magic all the world knows you possess, to learn something about the Swiss couriers and their whereabouts, and thus dispel half our doubts at once."

"Foolish boy! you think the secrets of magic are but a holiday trick?"

"Not so; but at this time, which you have yourself declared to be the climax, the gifts of each, be they great or small, should be freely contributed."

"Well reasoned," answered the alchemist; "and a process, which you and the world call magic, shall indeed be used when the time comes; it is for that and for nothing else I am here."

"But the time has already come when it might tell us what to expect, which all our conjectures cannot do."

"For that I have not by me indispensable appliances."

"Then we take the chance of their travelling by another route, or passing here without stopping,— in either case failure for us, and ruin for the duke."

"We must accept not only these two unfavorable possibilities, but half a dozen others far more serious."

"But in setting forth upon this expedition, and in making the declaration you did as to its results, you certainly must have had something more potent in view than anything of which you have yet spoken."

Almodoro looked about him to make sure that they were not observed. Then he said: "This grass is dry, now the sun has shone upon it; let us be seated, for the time has come when I may explain to you the method by which I intend to work, and the way in which you are to second me."

They placed themselves at ease upon the greensward that bordered the road, as though to enjoy the sunshine of the pleasant April afternoon, and the fragrance of apple blossoms that filled the air, and the delicious restfulness of the broad fields.

The alchemist spoke with a familiarity and confidence unusual to his distant and formal bearing.

"There exists," he said, fixing his dark eyes earnestly upon them, "a mysterious power in nature whereof I could give no rational explanation, even were it my present purpose to make the attempt. It is a strange and secret force which one person exercises upon another, whereby the consciousness and volition of the second are arrested."

His companions, filled with the universal dread of mystic influences, listened with undisguised astonishment and awe.

"This power," he continued, with difficulty restraining a smile at their timorous faces, "is a magnet with which phenomena can be produced that, to the natural sense, seem prodigies; the mind can be projected to distant places; communication can be held with those far away; the clue to things deemed unfathomable can be grasped; but what is of greater import to us is that the subject brought into the focus of the magnet—or magnetized, as it is called—can be made to do the bidding of him who exercises it, without afterwards retaining a remembrance of what he has been made to do."

He paused to note if this revelation produced an intelligible meaning upon minds unused to the science of alchemy. A glance exchanged by the young men satisfied him that the application to be made of this principle of the black art had been perceived by them, and the deference and intentness with which they listened showed that the witchery and intensity of their companion's nature had seized them.

He passed at once, and with a relieved expression, from the pale of the cabala to the commonplace of the service they were to render.

"It is upon this agency that I rely," he went

on, "and it is necessary that you be alert to divine my wish. You must be prompt to understand my slightest signal, and all that can be foreseen now is that I must have the bearer of our despatch to myself for half an hour; that I must be secure from interruption; that, above all, the superior must be kept out of the way."

A light footfall was heard on the road behind them.

"Hush," whispered Narvaez, hastily, "here comes the superior."

CHAPTER XIV.

AN ALCHEMIC MAGNET.

The prelate approached them with a fixed and scrutinizing eye. "I understand that you come from the French camp before Novara," he said, addressing Almodoro.

"Yes, we are sent to meet a bearer of important despatches."

"And are you French?"

"I am of many lands," replied the alchemist, vexed at this pointed inquiry.

"Your speech has a savor of Arabic," assented the Venetian. "And you," he said, addressing Narvaez, who was brushing the specks of dust from his doublet, "your dark skin bespeaks you a child of some southern province, of Gascony, perhaps, or —— ?"

"I am a Castilian," briefly responded the fencer, with the haughty accent of his race.

"And you," pursued the superior, turning to Hermes, "should also be a Spaniard, if my remembrance of costume be not at fault."

"I have spent much of my life among Spaniards," evasively answered Hermes, raising his handkerchief to his face in his desire to escape recognition.

Before they could be further questioned, the wise man hastily interposed.

"Twice since our arrival," he began, "I have sought an opportunity to reveal a hidden purpose connected with our journey, and if you and I could walk as far as the bend of the road——?"

The superior bowed in silent assent; he would willingly have pressed his interrogatory of the young men, but, finding no pretext for refusing the confidence of their chief, he followed.

"The magician will ruin all!" ejaculated Narvaez, looking vacantly after them.

"Fear not," answered Hermes, laughingly. "Though Almodoro talk much, he will tell little; I only wish he might play these monks some devil's trick,—set their thin blood boiling with fantastic lusts, or——"

"Tush, Hermes, for shame!"

"He has played wilder pranks than that."

"'Tis a marvel the Inquisition never put a tether about him."

"It sought to, years ago, but now that he is in high favor it dare not."

"How came it to fail? I thought the Holy Office never failed."

"It could never lay physical hands upon him, however much it scourged with ghostly stripes.

My uncle once told me an odd tale of how he escaped the Franciscans who had followed him for weeks ineffectually, till one night, as they dogged his steps, looking to see him vanish as usual in the wall of some house, or melt away into the shadow of a tree, he was seen to enter the palace where Ludovico then lived. A reinforcement of friars and a squad of halberdiers were summoned, and every door was guarded, and every window watched, while a search was commenced with swords and flambeaux and holy water. They ascended the stairs in a body, with exorcisms and clattering of sandals. Arrived at the portrait gallery, there came from its dim extremity a shuffling of limping footsteps, and they caught sight of the semblance of a lame old man in clerical habit, looking back with frightened face. It was Monsignore Pasquale, who was lame all his life, who had been dead twenty years, and whose life-size portrait hung on the wall. The friars raised a hue and cry at the sight, and rushed after like a rolling wave. But Ludovico, who had followed, turned instinctively to scan the Monsignore's likeness, and a chill crept over him on discovering that a different personage filled the picture. The wrinkled visage was replaced by a beautiful and intellectual head,— the head of Almodoro, and his body was robed in the magnificent garb of the doge Giacomo Contarini. The wizard had thrust the aged and infirm prelate from his place, and had substituted himself upon the board—himself as he was centuries ago! And when the monks and soldiers were weary with chasing shadows, they went their ways, and lo! next morning, Almodoro's image had vanished, and the Monsignore's had slunk back to its place. But look! the conjurer beckons us to him."

The alchemist and the superior had suddenly stopped by the roadside, and were looking northward, as though attracted by some expected sound. And Hermes and Narvaez, following their gaze, beheld two horsemen riding at a trot through the defile, both dressed in brown, the one wearing a light-colored felt hat, the other a peaked cap and feather.

The shaggy dogs came bounding out, with the stable facchini after them. To Almodoro's declaration that he had been sent by King Louis, the Swiss listened stolidly, nodding to one another and at him. And answering the superior, whose hand they reverently kissed, they told, in guttural dialect, of the road they had come, and how they had ridden, fasting, all that day over difficult mountain paths, and would rest the night and start again at dawn. And they acknowledged Almodoro's information to be correct, that one of them, named Soprasasso,—he with the leather doublet and gray hat,—bore a despatch to Ludovico, while his companion, who was referred to by the name of Caspar, must follow the road to the camp of King Louis. And being chilled, they seated themselves before a fire kindled in the refectory, and drew off their muddy boots and hung them upon the andirons to dry, and sat toasting their stockinged feet, and taking one or two gurgling draughts from a fiasco while waiting supper. And Hermes pledged them in a goblet, rejoicing that on the morrow they would have the trusty escort of himself and his companions, the roads being beset with cut-throats. And Almodoro scanned them intently: much the same build they were, and equipped alike, each with his courier's wallet and thick German cutlass laid on the table. But when he asked concerning their despatches, they answered nothing, nor did they exhibit anything but indifference at the promised escort. And when they were all served with ham, and bread and cheese, and eggs, the superior explained that, as the porter's lodge had already been occupied by Almodoro and his companions, the couriers should sleep in an ancient guard-room on the other side of the refectory, where two pallets had been laid for them on the floor.

The couriers eat ravenously, and, when their appetite was appeased, they returned drowsily to the fire and disposed themselves comfortably, like dogs that have hunted all day. The superior, finding no opportunity to speak a word to the Swiss apart, left the refectory at vespers, attended by Hermes, who promised himself not to let the suspicious prelate out of his sight. He doubted not that Narvaez would find an expedient to draw the courier named Caspar from the room, thus leaving Almodoro alone with the bearer of the coveted despatch.

The moment approached when the alchemist was to attempt an experiment which called for his most occult and potent science. He doubted not of its success, for the secrets of hypnotic magnetism had been divined and mastered by the fraternity, and Almodoro had developed the magnetic faculty to an extraordinary accuracy and range.

But, to the soothsayer's discomfiture, Soprasasso,—the one against whom his art was to be directed,—rose as the door closed behind Hermes, and declared it bedtime for himself and his companion.

"Come, Caspar," he said, giving that individual a nudge that made him open his sleepy eyes; "come and help me examine the fastenings; rouse up, man; do you not know we have but little over seven hours before us? and that is barely enough for a tolerable nap."

"I have several matters upon which to consult you," resolutely interposed Almodoro, determined to detain him; "send Caspar to examine the fastenings, and let us consider the route to your destination."

"The route is straight ahead," retorted the Swiss, upon whom Almodoro's advances had produced an unfavorable impression.

"But we have not even fixed the hour for starting," urged the alchemist, rising from his seat with a movement of impatience.

"We start at dawn," answered the courier, with a gesture of derision, "and if you must know more exactly, you have but to keep watch through the night;" and, taking a rushlight from the table, he opened the door that communicated with the adjoining guard-room, and closed it sharply behind him.

Narvaez followed his retreating figure with a look of blank dismay, but Almodoro had already found an alternative.

He caught Caspar by the arm as he made ready to follow, and, looking with good-natured earnestness in his face, said:

"Your mate has curt ways, and I like him, though not so well as you, for your wit is the keener, and your insight the more practical. With such a mind you will be to blame if you put not by a big sack of ducats to comfort your old age. If you will listen a moment, while Soprasasso is getting to bed, I will tell you a secret that will add a yellow handful to your savings."

"Speak it briefly then," muttered the Swiss; "I have no time for lengthy tales."

They seated themselves, side by side, before the fire, and Almodoro applied himself instantly, and with intense earnestness, to securing the attention and interest of the dull intelligence that listened.

"A courier's is a hard life," he said quickly,— "at least you should be well paid for such constant exposure."

"More copper than silver," answered Caspar sententiously, with the air of one who speaks a profound and melancholy truth.

"And I say I can put you in the way of something better than silver, if you will."

The courier rubbed his knees reflectively, and turned his heavy face full upon the alchemist with a look of silent interrogation.

"I can make your fortune; I need just such a trusty fellow as you for a delicate service where whoso can hold his tongue will be free to fill his pockets."

"What with?" asked the Swiss, losing interest in the fire.

"With ducats that have lain buried since the time of the first Visconti."

"And you know where they are hidden?"

"They are to be found by a divining-rod, which reveals treasure under ground as accurately as the eye perceives a light through the darkness."

"Do you offer me a handful of these ducats?"

"Yes, if you will do what I ask."

"And what is that?"

The voice of Soprasasso was heard calling angrily from the next room:

"To bed, Caspar, or I will put out the light!"

Almodoro whispered quickly: "Tell him to leave the light burning and to go to sleep; say that you will come in a moment."

When this answer had been made, the alchemist, dreading to see his prey escape, went on in a hurried undertone.

"Before I reveal all," he said, "you must pledge secrecy: put your hand in mine,—so,—look me straight in the eyes; speak not,—I shall believe you honest if you look upon me fixedly."

They sat thus hand in hand by the flickering logs, each with his eyes riveted upon the other's, the Swiss grown suddenly rigid, as though touched by a magnetic fire. Then his respiration quickened, his eyelids drooped, while behind leaned Narvaez, watching with beating heart what he doubted not to be a manifestation of the devil. During this interval a fantastic vision possessed the imagination of the Swiss. His fancy had been kindled by the last words spoken, and by the thought of the magical divining-rod; and now, for a single moment—which seemed an hour, so crowded was it with tumultuous and weird impressions— he beheld the conjurer walking at night, through strange and solitary places, in search of treasure, and finding it in stacks of curious and outlandish coin, and heaps of glittering gems, and piles of cups and sacred vessels; and behind all flitted lurid lights and demon faces, that suddenly grew dim as everything faded in a vague unconsciousness, across which the alchemist's next words came from a distance, with faint and solemn sound.

Several minutes passed; then Almodoro dropped the hand he held, and breathed a sigh of infinite relief.

"Fold your hands together," he said to the Swiss.

Instinctively the courier clasped them one upon the other.

"Stand up and walk to the window; do you see the window there before you?"

With a slow, hesitating action the order was performed.

" Give me the despatch from your wallet."

Caspar fixed his eyes vaguely upon the leather travelling-bag which lay upon the table; then with difficulty, as one who comprehends imperfectly what is required, he undid the strap and drew out a sealed envelope.

"Now put it back precisely as it was," said Almodoro, after a glance at the superscription. "You understand me when I speak?" he added, after this had been done.

"Yes, perfectly."

"Then tell me if your companion's wallet contains a letter similar to yours."

"He has the counterpart to mine," said Caspar, after a moment's intense thought, "but I cannot remember what is written upon it."

"And do you know what is in his letter or in yours?"

"They contain orders, but I know neither the words nor their meaning."

"Do you see objects about you?"

"I see you speaking to me."

"But do you not see this table and the fire?"

"Ah, yes; now I see them clearly."

"Have you been in the room in which you are to sleep?"

"I know not."

"It is the room beside this; see the door to it before us; it is there your companion, Soprasasso, awaits you."

"Soprasasso?"

"Yes; he who rides with you and carries a despatch."

"You are right; I know the man."

"I wish you to enter that room noiselessly, and to bring me Soprasasso's wallet."

The magnetized courier turned towards the door which had been indicated, and was about to approach it.

"Wait," interposed the alchemist; "I have not yet given you the information with which you must be prepared. On the floor of the adjoining room are two pallets. One is for you; the other is occupied by Soprasasso."

"Has he gone to bed?"

"Yes; but he will be sure to speak, and you must answer."

"What shall I say?"

"You are to answer thus: *Hush: make no noise: the monastery is asleep. I long to sleep, too—and so good-night until the morrow.*"

"Will I be able to see in that room?"

"Yes, because the rushlight has been left for you to put out."

"But where shall I find the wallet?"

"This youth who stands beside me has watched Soprasasso, and the wallet lies on the floor between the two beds. First put out the light; then lay your own wallet, which I put in your hands, on the floor, in the place of the one which now lies there, and which you are to bring to me very softly, as soon as Soprasasso sleeps. And remember that the instant you are in that room, you must bolt the door behind you. Do you understand it all clearly?"

"Not so clearly but that I would hear it again in order."

When the soothsayer had complied with this request, amplifying his instructions with extreme minuteness and precision of detail, the Swiss walked unhesitatingly to the door, went out, and closed and bolted it behind him.

"Master," exclaimed Narvaez, "would he now do anything that you command?"

"You see for yourself."

"Would he kill Soprasasso?"

"He would try if I bade him—with the probability of rousing the monastery; with the certainty of spoiling the most ingenious feature of our plan; and with the chance of being worsted after all."

The fencer looked unconvinced.

"It is necessary," pursued the wise man, as though speaking to himself, "that these fellows shall go on their way to-morrow unconscious that anything has befallen. How long the dunce takes!"

"Shall I listen at their door?"

"That were useless. If there be any noise—if Caspar fails, you will——"

"Listen. They are talking."

"No; it is a step. Hark, he draws back the bolt—he comes!"

The lights in the refectory had been extinguished, the fire burned low, all was dark and still. The door opened and Caspar entered, holding Soprasasso's wallet. Narvaez softly closed the door behind him, and the alchemist, undoing the straps, took the despatch to the fire, glanced at its contents with an exclamation of triumph, then dropped it in the midst of the embers, where it was instantly consumed.

The courier stood motionless and abstracted, as if his thoughts were not upon what was happening.

"Did Soprasasso speak?" asked Almodoro, while Narvaez strapped the wallet together.

"Yes; he chided me for tarrying so long."

"Was that all?"

"He bade me haste and put out the light. I answered as you charged me, and in the dark I laid my wallet in the place of his and came softly out."

"Very well. Now lay your wallet on the table beside your sword, and sit down by the fire. Give me your hand again."

At this moment Hermes reappeared and whispered that vespers were over, that he had tried in vain to detain the superior, and that they might be interrupted at any moment. Then he noticed with astonishment the courier's vague and blank expression, which gave place, as the magnetic influence was lifted, to his accustomed look of stolid attention. Almodoro spoke to him, resuming the thread of their talk at the point where it had been interrupted twenty minutes previously.

"You are an honest fellow," he said, "and, now I know you to be sincere, you may depend upon plunging your hands in the mounds of dingy red ducats, none the less beautiful to you and me for being tarnished."

"But when will you tell me wherein this service you require is to consist?" asked the Swiss, unconscious of the interval since the alchemist's reference to the divining-rod.

"It is late," answered Almodoro, impatient to get Caspar to his room. "To-morrow, as we ride, you shall learn all. Your companion went to bed some time ago—we had all best do likewise. Your shoes are dry now; take them with you, and give the remainder of the night to sleep."

The courier yawned, rose slowly, stretched himself luxuriously, took his boots from the andirons, and his wallet and cutlass from the table, and, bidding them all a curt good-night, withdrew.

Then Almodoro turned to Hermes, his face suffused with exultation. "It is done," he whispered, with trembling lips. "The despatch is destroyed."

"It is done none too soon," answered Hermes, "for the superior will surely be here in an instant. He fairly bade me begone at the last, and I know he suspects us of some mischievous intention."

"He can do no more than come to the refectory to make sure that all is quiet."

"Hark! I hear a step now," exclaimed Hermes, breathless with excitement.

"Some one knocks at the door of the Swiss. It is the superior. He has something to say to them, and we must know what it is."

They crept to the door leading to the guardroom, and listened intently. The first words they heard were spoken by Caspar, who had relighted the rush he had previously extinguished, and was opening the side-door at which the superior knocked. Soprasasso, roused by these noises, threw back his coverlet with an angry growl. Then they heard the superior speaking in a quick, subdued voice.

"I come," he said, "to caution you against these fellows who present themselves under the guise of an escort. Is your door bolted? Yes? Know, then, that one of them is Hermes Sforza, nephew to the Duke of Milan. I met him once, months ago, in Venice, but he is so altered that at first I knew him not. As for his companions, though they profess to come from the French camp, you see for yourselves that neither of them is a Frenchman. All day they have been studying the ins and outs of this building, and never for an instant have their arms been out of reach. This afternoon, when I came upon them unawares, their chief, who is the oldest and most ill-favored of them, palmed off a tale whose falsehood looked me in the eyes. And I should have been here earlier to tell you this, had not the one whom I recognized, when talking face to face, as Sforza, detained me with a tissue of nonsense."

The Swiss evinced little concern at this extraordinary communication, which they attributed to the disordered imagination of a monk.

"I have but this moment left them dozing over their fire," observed Caspar. "And we have nothing to lose except our despatches," he added, with a sigh at the remembrance of Almodoro's treasure.

"Except your despatches," echoed the superior.

"And they are as they should be," added Soprasasso, turning to the two wallets beside him with a searching glance that changed to a wild stare of alarm.

His hands shook as he clutched his own and held it up for the others to see.

"It has been opened," he stammered. "I never fastened it thus."

The superior bent above him as he unstrapped it and found it empty.

"The despatch!" he cried, with a terrible voice, as he beat his hands violently together.

His companion looked on bewildered, then suddenly tore open his own wallet and drew forth the despatch it contained to the auxiliaries of King Louis.

At sight of it Soprasasso gasped with joy.

"St. Michael, the guardian of messengers, be praised!" he muttered, as he clutched the parchment and pressed it to his lips. "We can yet perform our errand," he said, "for the other despatch was the mate to this, and both recall our countrymen to Switzerland."

On the other side of the door Almodoro stood silent and aghast at the words. Behind him were Hermes and Narvaez, and they read their failure in the eyes with which he glanced back.

Then the superior spoke again. "These fellows must have stolen the letter at supper before your very faces," he said. "This is no place for you to sleep; they will get the second from you before morning. You must to horse at once. Come, I will guide you to the stable. The facchini are not yet in bed. We must show no light, for they are better armed than you. Pull on your boots, take your cutlasses, and follow me softly."

A shuffling noise followed, then all was still. The superior went but a step with them outside the walls. Then he whispered: "The stable is open, you can easily saddle your horses. Meanwhile I will go to the parapet, and, if the rogues stir, I will ring the great bell."

Within the refectory Almodoro turned to his companions and asked in a calm, deliberate voice, "Are your weapons ready?"—then, without waiting for an answer, he added: "You must be quick to seize our last chance. The superior has marred a finer scheme than ever he made. But you are cool and bold, and your arms are good. You must kill Soprasasso. He was to have ridden to our camp. He is intelligent enough to make explanations, which the other is not. Caspar will ride to Louis' camp and deliver his despatch. Whoever approaches our Swiss shall be hanged as a spy. Come quickly; you will know them readily in the dark, for Soprasasso's hat will show almost white, and will make a clear target. Be sure not to fire at the other. You shall station yourselves before the stable door, and I will lock the monastery gate, that none may come out to molest you."

Softly they passed from the refectory, where the neglected fire burned low, casting their shadows in grotesque and fantastic silhouettes upon the wall. The stout old boards creaked beneath their steps as Hermes led the way with a pistol in each hand, and at his heels the fencer holding the redoubtable blunderbuss. The alchemist locked the great gate behind them and leaned against it, completely hidden in shadow, while his companions stepped forward to the edge of the road.

The double doors of the stable were opened; they heard the noise of horses led forth; a head peeped cautiously this way and that; there was a hasty exchange of words; then, with a rush, the Swiss were upon them, cutlass in hand.

Two sharp reports rang out, followed by the louder detonation of the blunderbuss, and one of the Swiss—the one wearing the light gray hat—plunged headlong to the ground. The other spurred furiously, and, in passing Narvaez, dealt him a heavy cut ere he dashed away at a gallop.

It was over in an instant. Then Almodoro came forward as Hermes sprang to the Spaniard, who had fallen. Along the rampart came hurrying lights, and the monastery bell rang a note of alarm far down the valley.

"What!" exclaimed the alchemist, bending beside Narvaez, "is she killed?"

"*She!*" echoed Hermes.

"Did you not know your fencer to be a girl? She is badly hurt. The cut has gone through the arm to the bone. Give me a handkerchief,—there, bound thus the flow of blood will cease. Look, her eyes open, she tries to speak. How the monks swarm on the parapet. Hear them curse,—no, they are praying. Let us get the horses, quick, and away!"

CHAPTER XV.

THE FAITH OF THE SWISS.

At daybreak Hermes and the wounded girl neared Novara. Almodoro had disappeared soon after their flight from the monastery, for the alchemist was in dire haste, and made off at a pace which left them far behind.

At intervals, during the hours of their long ride, they talked with a strange mixture of intimacy and reserve, and by degrees Hermes drew forth the story of her life. She spoke with horror of that dreadful man who had divined her secret, and, in place of the fencer's accustomed self-reliance, appeared a sudden feminine dependence, wherewith in her helplessness she turned to her companion, and which was in odd contrast to the epithets that, in moments of pain, she showered upon their thorny journeyings.

Her name, she said, was Mariquita, and her disguise had been imagined by her father, who, when she was still a child, dressed her as a boy, and put a foil in her hand, saying that she must take the place of the son he had desired. At his death he had enjoined upon her to continue the life to which she had become accustomed, and, committing to her his Toledo blade, which, in its youth, had tasted the blood of many a Moor, whispered his last characteristic words: "To the heart! always strike to the heart!"—then his eyes closed, he was dead.

She interrupted this narrative with denunciations of the alchemist, with lamentations that she should never fence again, with sobs of pain, with wondering exclamations at what should become of her now. At which Hermes, thinking to calm her, said:

"I will care for you, Mariquita, until you can be safely placed in a convent—a shrewish nun you will make!"

At this the long-familiar masculine nature reasserted itself, and the fencer's daughter vowed by the sword of St. Peter that none should ever house her in a nunnery.

When nearing camp, they heard from afar the soft, musical notes of the mountain horns wherewith the Swiss sounded their reveillé, and whose simple refrain, swelling and falling in the distance, seemed filled with the pastoral strains of Alpine valleys. And, following after, came the roll of drums and the strident call of bugles from the French and Italian camps. They passed Ludovico's outposts almost unchallenged, and rode through the familiar bivouac, where every-

thing wore an aspect of bustling preparation.
In an adjacent meadow were formed the Italian
knights, silent and motionless, glittering beneath
the first beams of the rising sun, in the steel
and brass of their incomparable Milanese armor.
Near by, the crossbowmen, in dark green tunics
and feathered caps, were filling their wallets with
bolts, and, away to the left, a battalion of Lombard pikemen advanced with trumpet-blasts and
clashing of Turkish cymbals.

Hermes conducted Mariquita to a house occupied by a leech, in whose care he left her. He
then rode to Ludovico's tent, before which Sanseverino was seated on horseback, surrounded by
officers, to whom he was reading his order for an
attack. A little to the front was Sforza, equipped
in gilt mail, and attended by an esquire who bore
his shield, rather in observance of ancient custom
than in view of any heavy strokes the portly duke
was likely to receive or give. Beside him rode
Almodoro, whose usually sombre countenance was
radiant, as though success were the elixir of his
being.

But the promised triumph vanished at the startling words of some officers who galloped in with
blanched faces and trembling lips, and whose tidings struck the alchemist and his patron equally
aghast. The Swiss had furled their flags and
called in their sentries, and were busy with their

lansquenettes rolling tents and packing baggage, and refused to obey orders, declaring that a command from a source superior to the authority of princelings called them away.

It needed but a moment to verify this statement, and to measure the immensity of the catastrophe. They rode forward to the lines of their mercenaries, where Ludovico was greeted with derisive shouts.

"You promised us Vigevano; you promised us Novara," they cried; "you shall learn to keep faith with the Swiss."

Then Hermes whispered to Almodoro: "We made some fatal mistake last night; can it be that the Swiss we killed was the one sent to the French camp? See how pale is Ludovico! what can it be they are saying to him?—they unfold a despatch——"

"I cannot bear to meet his eyes," groaned the wise man; "I am faint,—the sight of his face oppresses me."

"Look yonder!" exclaimed Hermes, catching the alchemist by the sleeve and directing his attention: "that fellow pointing to us—do you not recognize him?—it is Soprasasso. I understand it all now: in the haste of their flight the one took the other's hat. Him we riddled with bullets had caught up his companion's gray felt— O Magician, to what purpose are your arts?"

But Ludovico, at least, did not despair. He could escape with his Italian troops to Milan, and defend his capital until a duplicate despatch reached the hirelings of King Louis, and left that sovereign similarly denuded. For this a little time was necessary, that a few miles might be gained unmolested. He rode forward to reconnoitre the French lines, and perceived with dismay the menacing activity which evidenced that the enemy were aware of the collapse of his army, and would be quick to profit by it.

Meanwhile the Swiss till now in his service continued their preparations for departure, undisturbed by the approach of the enemy, who, having driven in the Italian outposts, halted as though anticipating some concerted event. And while they waited thus, one of the chiefs of Ludovico's Swiss, named Sileno of Uri, was addressed by Soprasasso the courier, whose services were so well known and so valued that, upon his request, Sileno led him a few paces apart.

"The moment accorded to me upon my arrival was so brief," began Soprasasso, "and my tidings were so great, that I could not tell you of the snare set for me last night."

"What matters it now, since you escaped?"

"But my companion did not. Poor Caspar! I heard the shots fired by those who surrounded us; I saw him fall. Master, I no longer doubt that my life-long comrade was cruelly done to death."

"Your own skin is whole; what more asks a man whose days and nights are equally spent in danger?"

"Revenge!" answered the courier, with a violent gesture, as though he crushed the skull of a foe with his fist.

"Holy Virgin!" ejaculated Sileno, surprised at the other's ferocity, "am I to scour the valleys of the Alps to find some rogues with whom you brawled?"

"They are here beneath your hand. I saw them following the duke a moment ago. The youth who fired upon us is Sforza's nephew, and he with the lowering brow is a conjuring worker of charms."

"For a nephew of the duke we shall extort a rich ransom," replied Sileno, with his broad face aglow. "I see your drift, good Soprasasso; you require a consolation for the shots fired last night. Fear not; you shall have a sequin for every bullet,—say three—or shall we say four in all?"

The courier waved aside this magnanimous offer. "I want no sequins," he retorted angrily, "nor can you need more than the French will pay for this day's work. For myself, I require those two men's lives, nor will aught else content me."

"What reckless waste! King Louis would pay a thousand crowns for young Sforza."

"He is worth more than that to me dead."

"If you are thus spendthrift, you will come to want in your old age."

"Refuse me not. Or, rather, remember I could tell the Diet things you would pay well to have unspoken."

"Hush! I meant but to see if your zeal were to be trusted. You shall have the youth, and the conjurer too, since nothing else will serve."

"Good," answered the courier, with a sardonic laugh; "and they must be delivered in such convenient way as I shall fix."

The officer stopped to reflect upon this demand, holding his cap in his hands and adjusting its blue heron's plume. Then he said in a low voice:

"I go presently to the duke. I can make a proposal of escape for his nephew which will bring him in your way."

"And the magician?"

"Father of usurers! You ask much of my patience."

"No matter, then; you shall send me the youth alone, whither I designate."

"And where is that to be?"

"Tell him that in the clump of trees to the left, yonder, near that burned house, he will find one who for twenty ducats will guide him safely beyond the enemy's line."

"But if he goes there with a man or two, and finds you, he will finish what he began last night."

"Fear not. I shall make bold to borrow half a dozen of your fellows of Uri, and it will go hard if we cannot turn the tables."

"Do you mean that you will kill him?"

"As surely as there is a man to follow me, or a blade wherewith to strike."

Sileno shrugged his shoulders at the uselessness of further argument, and rejoined his battalion. It was not long before he walked across the interval which separated the bivouac of his soldiers from the duke's tent. The sentry had left his post, and he entered unannounced.

Ludovico had thrown off his helmet and gauntlets, and was sitting, still clad in glittering splendor, with downcast eyes. On hearing a step he looked up, and his face lighted with scornful indignation at sight of Sileno.

The Swiss was disconcerted by the silent disdain of his gaze. He came prepared for threats, for reproaches, for entreaty; but that mute abhorrence pierced to the very baseness of his soul. He was about to withdraw when Il Moro spoke.

"What purpose," he asked bitterly, "brings you now to intrude upon me?"

The hireling's self-sufficiency returned at the words.

"Signor Duca," he answered, "I bear ill news: the enemy's cavalry has circled round Novara; it is too late for flight, and a flag has come in demanding your surrender."

"What concerns it you if flags are sent,—you whose battle-flags are furled?"

"Because, while the time for fighting has passed, there remains one last chance of escape."

"Escape, then, and glory in your flight."

"But you, Signor Duca, - your own safety; you have not heard the enemy's conditions!"

"I have heard nothing since I listened to the order bidding you abandon me."

"And your life, is that nothing? Trivulzio's terms are these: that we, in obedience to the Diet, march off unmolested. That your Italian soldiers be disarmed and disbanded. And for you, that you yield yourself prisoner at discretion, mercy or no mercy."

A shadow passed over Sforza's eyes.

"Ay, there speaks Trivulzio," he answered, after a moment's silent agony.

"But he can be outwitted," pursued Sileno, catching at Ludovico's distress. "Why should not you go with us unnoticed, and so reach some place of friendly safety?"

"I could not go a hundred paces undetected; besides, how can I trust the faith of the Swiss?"

"The faith of the Swiss is worth as much as the promises you broke at Vigevano and Novara."

"I had rather venture out in arms with my Italian knights than to trudge away shoulder to shoulder with you lanzknechts, wearing the cloak that covers your shame."

At this taunt the Swiss turned with an impetuous look towards the door. "The Italian knights!" he echoed, with outstretched arms,—"where are they? I saw them charge the famous regiment *Auvergne* an hour ago, and that charge not only failed, but wrecked them."

"Then I will ride straight to King Louis and yield me, as misfortune may yield without dishonor."

"You forget," objected Sileno coldly, "that you are outlawed for treason to the arms of France, and that Louis will not hearken to your plea."

At this ominous reminder the unhappy prince drew a handkerchief across his brow and answered not.

"Come," said the Swiss, seating himself familiarly at the duke's side; "in this extremity we will do you a good turn as amends for the order which no power of ours could change. At least you can escape an ignominious death,—bethink you, the hangman's rope before the eyes of the whole French army."

"Your column marches at once?"

"Immediately."

"And the disguise?"

"Listen," replied the Swiss, speaking in an undertone, and laying his finger upon his lips with an affectation of mystery. "In place of this armor put on the cowl of one of our friars, and mount upon one of the donkeys they ride. Not even my own men will know you, and at sunset we shall be beyond reach."

Mariquita's last impression, when Hermes left her, and when she composed herself to sleep upon the veranda where the leech had bidden her rest, was of brilliant sunlight, and of a multitude of pink roses trellised against the wall, and of an exquisite freshness and fragrance in the air. And in the deep slumber that followed, her adventurous journey was forgotten, and she dreamt of the lattice window from which, in infancy, she looked upon the Castilian sierras, and upon a prim, rectangular garden whose venerable hedge of box stretched away in solemn and odorous fringe. And she remembered playing as a child in that garden, and wondered now, in her dream, whether some day, years hence, she might revisit those familiar walks, and recall, in the silver twilight of life, the places where grew the golden roses of her youth.

And she still slept when Hermes returned. Il

Moro had profited by his opportunity of escape; Sileno of Uri had indicated to the duke's nephew the means of flight destined to lead him into Soprasasso's ambuscade; the horses were ready, the moments passing—they must be gone at once.

But as Hermes stood beside Mariquita, the current of her dream altered. Her features became contracted, and she spoke aloud in a voice that was changed and weak, coming, as it seemed, across an infinite distance of anguish and remorse.

"*When she is lost and ruined,*" she muttered, "*she will gladly give herself to death.*"

At these sinister words Hermes drew back the hand outstretched to wake her.

"*How often I have seen her dead face,*" went on the girl, with a moan of weariness, "*and to think that I saw her living but once.*"

The listener bent forward to catch the words. A strange suspicion seized him, and his face became haggard as that of the sleeping girl. Once more she spoke:

"*Dead!*" she ejaculated: "*is she dead? I know not,—none knows but he.*"

Then she woke with a violent start, glanced wildly about her at the unfamiliar objects, and met Hermes' accusing gaze.

She raised herself with a gasp of terror, and would have caught his hand, but he motioned her back and asked:

"Who is it that alone knows if she be dead?"

But the horror of her dream and the bewilderment of her awakening left the girl dazed, and she answered his question with another.

"She!—who is she?"

"Bianca Rucellai."

At this name, which she heard spoken by Hermes for the first time since she had delivered her rival to dishonor, Mariquita cowered with the helpless fright of one whose awful misdeed is discovered.

Her fear and her silence told the story of her crime.

"And he who knows if she be dead or not," pursued Hermes steadily, "is Valentino? You start at the name, for it recalls your own infamy as well as his. Oh Mariquita!" he exclaimed with eyes suffused, "how could you, whom I thought my most faithful friend, do me a wrong that even an enemy would hardly have inflicted?"

"Because I loved you," answered the girl, speaking with sudden strength and vehemence that melted to a paroxysm of sobs. "Have pity! you were all the world to me—I once risked my life for you: I would give the blood of my heart for you now. A hundred times it has been on my lips to tell you the secret that has racked me."

"And that was a token of your love, to deliver my helpless and innocent sweetheart to the lust of a fiend! And you have carried this coward's secret in your heart, and taken my hand in yours, and smiled in my face—you, that, were you a man, would not now be alive to hear me."

At these words Mariquita wept no more. The decisive instant of her life had come, and she dashed away her tears, impatient of such weakness. And from her suffering and exhaustion she lifted to Hermes her face filled with the intense persuasion of feminine entreaty, and outstretched her arms with appealing and infinite tenderness.

"Can you fancy us parted," she cried, "one from the other forever? Or can you turn away with indifference, and leave me to the loneliness of the world? Think, before you forsake me, how vital is this instant! Think how insignificant, hereafter, compared to your decision, will seem half the things in life! To me, all on earth but you seems a futile shadow, and in this hour, when, perhaps, the bitterness of death draws near, I think only of the greater pang of my punishment, and I look beyond my fault, and pray that in another world I may be judged more mercifully— even by you."

A step was heard as she spoke, and the leech stood before them, attracted by their voices, and looked from one to the other. And he caught Mariquita's wounded arm and replaced it in a sling, and took her by the shoulders and laid her down upon the cane sofa, and begged her to be quiet; but she broke from him with an inarticulate cry: "Hermes, Hermes, come back; forgive me!" Then she looked about her in silence.

He was gone—gone from her forever.

He rode at a canter, hardly thinking whither he went—past groups returning to Novara, and servants and sutlers hurrying this way and that, and stragglers wandering in an aimless fashion that betrayed their quest for plunder. Already, in the tacit truce that prevailed, the French officers were riding up to reconnoitre. But now the Swiss were in movement, and the head of their column had some time since passed between the line of French drawn up on either side of the highway. The departure of the mercenaries was evidently a subject of extreme interest, for Amboise, and Trivulzio, and D'Aubigny, and Ives d'Allègre, and all but King Louis himself, were there to see it. And at this distant spectacle Hermes, knowing the manner of the duke's evasion, drew bridle to watch if indeed he escaped. But even as he halted there was a break in the marching line, a figure on a donkey was dragged from the ranks, the friar's cowl was torn from his head—then the Swiss resumed their way. They had fulfilled their bargain with the enemy, and Sileno of Uri, stepping forward to Trivulzio, interrupted that officer's sarcastic welcome to the captive, and exclaimed:

"The money, oh greatest of men—the thirty thousand crowns. Are they ready?"

From the place where Hermes had stopped he could see Ludovico standing before the group of French officers, though too far to distinguish else but that. Then, remembering his appointed trysting-place, he rode away in the direction of the clump of trees, all unconscious of the fate that lurked there.

But, as he went, the quick gallop of a horse was heard behind, and glancing back, he perceived Le Chevalier Bayard, equipped in the armor wherewith he had once before been made familiar, though now with vizor raised, and with no weapon in the hand he waved in salutation, and upon his feet the great spurs of knighthood which had rewarded his prowess before Milan.

"I was riding to look at your camp," he said, with courtly greeting, as Hermes drew bridle, "and recognized you from afar. I wish to bid you God-speed, and to see you safe out of reach of your hirelings."

Then Hermes thanked him, and, pointing to the trees a bowshot distant, said that one waited there who had promised to conduct him beyond the French vedettes. And, as he spoke, both caught sight of Soprasasso and his men peering from behind the branches and trying to conceal their long, keen halberds.

The French knight divined their purpose, and addressed them with characteristic force and brevity. As the Swiss skulked sullenly away, he asked, with ironical deference:

"Were these the good friends who promised to see you harmless?"

"You have saved me!" ejaculated Hermes. Then, with a sudden anguish, he added: "Yet am I wretched enough to have welcomed the end."

"And shared the duke's imprisonment!" exclaimed Le Bayard, misunderstanding his thought. "Then you would have deprived me of the privilege of repaying something of Sforza's generosity. For him, in this pass, an obscure officer can do nothing; but, in a service to you, I acquit my debt to the utmost of my power. Ride straight on. We are at the flank of the French camp. Our cavalry is far from here. You have not a moment to lose, nor have I."

The sky, which had been overcast for an hour, suddenly brightened as Hermes cast a parting glance at the house, half a mile behind, where he had abandoned Mariquita. In that instant's change the earth became covered with a radiance of sunshine, and the heavens seemed filled with ineffable peace. And as swift as that transition from shadow to brightness, came a revulsion over the man, who lingered and hesitated in the act of snatching the proffered freedom.

"I cannot leave her," he murmured; "I will share her fate."

And with a nod of farewell to his astonished rescuer, he galloped back to the veranda where Mariquita still lay, beneath the trellised roses, in the breathless swoon of her despair.

CONCLUSION.

At evening on the day of the surrender, Ludovico Sforza was immured in the castle of Novara. De Ligny caused the fallen duke to be treated with commiseration, and to be furnished with suitable clothing in the place of the friar's disguise.

King Louis refused to see the captive, and presently passed sentence of perpetual confinement in the French dungeon of La Pierre Encise. The journey towards the Alps was slow; the prisoner suffering such paroxysms of anguish, as the cavalcade drew further from all that he had lost, that, fearing he would not survive, the escort tarried at places by the way, to break the final pang of passing beyond sight of Italy. At length they entered a narrow valley; the vegetation became sparse; only a glimpse remained of some white specks of houses beside a campanile tower, and the distant green, and the southern sunshine,—then he noticed nothing until, at Lyons, he was led through the midst of the jeering populace.

Six months' reclusion followed in La Pierre Encise. One morning, profiting by an inattention of some guards, he slipped, unnoticed, into a cart that was presently to be driven out of the courtyard, and concealed himself beneath the straw with which it was filled.

Once outside, he walked through the woods all that long summer's day, making slow progress and little heeding whither he went. At evening he came to water, and threw himself face downward, drinking deep, and dipping his parched hands in the running stream. And when the stars became visible he laid his course towards Lyons, intending to beg food and shelter. But he soon became exhausted, and fell asleep at a place where he stopped to rest.

A fine rain was falling when he woke—chilled, stiff, and footsore. He gathered a handful of wild berries, and, hearing the tramp of horses and the voices of men, knew that his pursuers were near. He lay hidden among some bushes until these sounds ceased, and then ventured forward. At dusk, being faint and half delirious with hunger, and seeing the light of a woodman's cottage, he walked to it in desperation and besought a crust of its inmates. And they smiled and set provision before him, but, shrewdly guessing this starving wanderer to be the fugitive for whom the country was scoured, one of them slipped away unnoticed, and at the moment Ludovico rose to pursue his wanderings, the cottage was surrounded.

Warned by this escape, he was removed to a place of greater security, the castle of Lys Saint

Georges, where he remained four years. In 1506 he was transferred to the fortress of Lorches, in Touraine, which as lately as 1720 was entire, even to the frescoes and sentences which Sforza painted on the walls of his chamber, and which are detailed by the pen of a visitor in that year. Refused the solace of writing materials, he asked for and obtained colors and brushes, and applied himself to painting on the half-lighted walls of his cell. His eyes accustomed themselves to the obscurity, and he created a pastime wherewith to struggle against the sad and heavy days. In the infinite desolation and despair of his living death, he delighted to recall the scenes of his earlier years, and traced upon the walls silhouettes and outlines that doubtless, in his hours of reverie, appeared to him as real as life. These sketches are described as finished with the elaboration of a hand that seeks to beguile the hours; all were stamped with a character and force that laid in pathetic imagery upon the rough plaster the costumes and processions and landscapes of that Italy the captive was to behold no more. The most remarkable was a life-size head of himself wearing an iron casque and surrounded by the words:

Je m'arme de patience.

The features represented a vigorous soldier, with dark eyes, heavy, sombre eyebrows, aquiline nose, full lower lip, and sharply-defined chin. At one side was the legend:

Qui ne craint Fortune n'est pas sage !

Year after year went by. All hope of release or of escape faded; communication by letter was, from the first, refused; he learned only at long intervals that his children were in Germany; that Isabelle lived in seclusion at Bari; that her son Francesco had been made Abbot of Nourmentiers, where he was learning to forget the ties of the world.

Year after year went by. Every day an officer looked in at the grated door, and at morning and evening came an old menial with food; sometimes the latter paused to talk—to enumerate his aches and infirmities, and to bewail the hardships of his poverty-stricken age: "Life is full of grievous changes," he was wont to say; then, with a sigh, he murmured, "*and sorrow is so much more intense than joy!*"

At first Ludovico took exact note of time, marking each day with a scratch, and Sundays with a tiny cross, until the bitterness of their lengthening line exceeded the gratitude of counting the passage of weeks and months. They showed no progress towards release, and he wearied of them. But while he thus lost the record of his imprisonment, he could tell each

Sunday by the chanting of priests in the chapel, and no festival passed unnoticed, for, leaning at his dark and narrow casement, he heard the sound of merry voices, and the laughter, and the songs of love and war, and knew that others were light-hearted. Looking by day from his turret, he saw waving tree-tops and drifting clouds, and heard from unseen pastures the faint, sweet tinkling of cow-bells. The solitude and the dull routine continued, the outer world grew more and more remote, and even the sting of his reverses became less poignant. His mind assumed a retrospective habit, and he thought often of his early years, and of the forest paths of his youth, which took on now the semblance of enchanted ground—like the sunny meadows which sometimes haunt a winter night's dream. But, even in thinking of the Past, the gruesome Present smote him with the words of his boding jailer—*sorrow is so much more intense than joy*. And the seasons in their course succeeded each other, the December snow and whistling wind: the morning-glory creeping in spring-time to his lofty window, and caressing the stone with tremulous leaves; in summer the birds chirping through the cool branches, or flitting to the free expanse of the fields; in autumn the voices of the peasants rising from neighboring vineyards—as year after year went by.

Until one day, the 10th of August, 1512, the door

was opened and an officer appeared, who, with smiling face and reverent salutation, invited Ludovico to the presence of the governor. Ten years' solitary confinement in the half-twilight of mediæval dungeons had made him a feeble and broken man, and he followed with slow and heavy step, and with spirit dejected and eyes grown dim, and the beautiful long hair gray and matted, and the common clothes his jailers allowed him threadbare and neglected. And as they passed the flower beds before the governor's house, the gardener, trimming a bed of plants, turned from his work, and, tossing his cap to the ground, advanced with obeisance, and offered Ludovico a spray of honeysuckle, with the single word " Monseigneur." Sforza took the flower, muttered an abstracted syllable of thanks, and looked with surprise at the man who spoke, for the first time, with the old familiar homage.

The governor and his assembled lieutenants rose from their seats as he entered, and their first words pierced his heart with a throb of such profound emotion that the blood surged to his brain and the room swam before his eyes. In that single instant he touched a whole long gamut of tears and ecstasy, of sadness and exultation. The officers gathered about, placed him in the governor's chair, and held to his lips a goblet of the generous wine of Burgundy. They bade him take courage and summon a great spirit, for he was free now,—not only free, but restored to his duchy. He listened in a dull stupor as the words were explained: King Louis had met with reverses in Italy, and the most effective counterstroke was to liberate the Duke of Milan, give him means to appeal to the popular faction, and thereby deprive the Spaniards of what their prowess had wrested from the French.

Ludovico collected himself, rose from his chair, and with trembling lips thanked them for their good tidings and kindly auguries. And, standing before them in his shabby dress, there came to him again the courtly pride, and the conscious power, and the kindling look of the brilliant days of his prime. And he said to them: "You are strangers to me, or rather should I say that you are new-found friends; forgive me, then, if, in this hour of overwhelming emotion, my soul turns with yearning to my beloved companions of old. Suffer me to walk an hour through the fields—perchance the image of some of them will rise to greet me."

And the governor made way, and led as far as the drawbridge, and the duke went out alone between the sentinels. He strolled aimlessly across the quiet meadows, where the bees were busy amid the clover, and inhaled the freshness of the free and fragrant air. It seemed to him the most beautiful day of his life. His eyes delighted in the glancing sheen of the river, the hazy clumps of willows, the suave and graceful outline of the hills. Regrets, and lamentations, and self-reproach were all forgotten now in the thrill of life reclaimed, and in presence of the throng of aspirations and resolves that sprang to salute him.

At a bend in the way, beneath a cluster of pines, was the God's-acre of a neighboring village, and, sauntering by, he stopped to lean at the fence and to look upon the wooden crosses crumbling to dust, and headstones bent awry, which marked where slept those who once were the youths and girls of the village green. And, fatigued by the tumult of this tremendous day, he seated himself by the wayside. His head sank, and tears gathered in his eyes, for tears had been familiar through so long suffering that they came now, even in the hour of unmeasured happiness. And so, beneath the deep shadows of the breathless pines, and amid the intense silence of the summer afternoon, he gazed for the last time upon the pathos and the glory of the sunset. And, as he looked, an infinite exhaustion dulled his thoughts, and a chill stole over the sunshine, and all the pleasant things of earth faded into dimness. And there they found him soon after,—dead and at rest. A sudden ecstasy, stronger than the prolonged grief of years, had broken his heart. For once, *joy had been more intense than sorrow.*

www.ingramcontent.com/pod-product-compliance
Lightning Source LLC
Chambersburg PA
CBHW031336230426
43670CB00006B/346